ntury 21

SOUTH-WESTERN

Accounting 9E

Multicolumn Journal
Working Papers TE, Chs. 17–24

Claudia Bienias Gilbertson, CPA
Teaching Professor
North Hennepin Community College
Brooklyn Park, Minnesota

Mark W. Lehman, CPA
Associate Professor
School of Accountancy
Mississippi State University
Starkville, Mississippi

SOUTH-WESTERN
CENGAGE Learning™

Australia · Brazil · Canada · Mexico · Singapore · Spain · United Kingdom · United States

SOUTH-WESTERN
CENGAGE Learning™

Working Papers Teacher's Edition, Chs. 17-24,
Multicolumn Journal, Century 21 Accounting, 9E

Claudia Bienias Gilbertson, CPA;
Mark W. Lehman, CPA

VP/Editorial Director: Jack W. Calhoun
VP/Editor-in-Chief: Karen Schmohe
VP/Director of Marketing: Bill Hendee
Sr. Marketing Manager: Courtney Schulz
Marketing Coordinator: Gretchen Wildauer
Marketing Communications Manager: Terron Sanders
Production Manager: Patricia Matthews Boies
Content Project Manager: Diane Bowdler
Consulting Editor: Bill Lee
Special Consultants: Sara Wilson, Robert E. First
Manufacturing Buyer: Kevin Kluck
Production Service: LEAP Publishing Services, Inc.
Compositor: GGS Book Services
Cover Designer: Nick & Diane Gliebe, Design Matters
Cover Images: Getty Images, Inc.

ISBN-13: 978-0-538-44713-3
ISBN-10: 0-538-44713-3

South-Western Cengage Learning
5191 Natorp Boulevard
Mason, OH 45040
USA

Cengage Learning products are represented in Canada by Nelson Education, Ltd.

For your course and learning solutions, visit **school.cengage.com**

THE TEACHER'S EDITION

The Teacher's Edition of the *Working Papers* for Chapter 17–Appendix A of CENTURY 21 ACCOUNTING, 9E contains the same forms as the Student's Edition, but all the solutions are overprinted in bold italic type. Solutions are given in the Teacher's Edition for (1) Study Guides, (2) Work Together Exercises, (3) On Your Own Exercises, (4) Application Problems, (5) Mastery Problems, (6) Challenge Problems, (7) Source Document Problems, and (8) Reinforcement Activity 3.

Although forms are provided for both the Mastery Problem and Challenge Problem at the end of a chapter, it is recommended that only one of these problems be assigned, according to the needs of the student. The solutions appear in this Teacher's Edition in the same sequence as the problems are presented in the Student's Edition.

PREPARING TRANSPARENCIES WITH THE TEACHER'S EDITION

Any page of this Teacher's Edition may be used as a master for making a transparency for use with the overhead projector. For best results, follow the instructions of the manufacturer of the transparency materials and the copying equipment being used in your school. Occasionally, because of the age of the materials or the equipment, some experimentation in making transparencies may be necessary.

This Teacher's Edition has been 3-hole-punched so that it may be placed in the Teacher's Resource Binder.

Printed in the United States of America
2 3 4 5 6 7 14 13 12

Study Guide 17

Name	Perfect Score	Your Score
Analyzing Uncollectible Accts. Expense and Allowance for Uncollectible Accts.	20 Pts.	
Analyzing Uncollectible Accounts Receivable	8 Pts.	
Journalizing Adjustments for Uncollectible Accounts Expense	12 Pts.	
Total	40 Pts.	

Part One—Analyzing Uncollectible Accounts Expense and Allowance for Uncollectible Accounts

Directions: Place a *T* for True or an *F* for False in the Answers column to show whether each of the following statements is true or false.

	Answers
1. A business generally sells on account to encourage sales. (p. 514)	1. *T*
2. Accounts receivable that cannot be collected are called uncollectible accounts. (p. 514)	2. *T*
3. Allowing customers to buy now and pay later is an ineffective method for increasing sales. (p. 515)	3. *F*
4. The amount of accounts receivable that is uncollectible is an expense. (p. 515)	4. *T*
5. A business usually knows at the end of the fiscal year which customer accounts will become uncollectible. (p. 515)	5. *F*
6. Allowance for Uncollectible Accounts is a contra account to its related asset account, Accounts Receivable. (p. 515)	6. *T*
7. Recording an estimate of uncollectible accounts to the contra asset account and the expense account is an application of the Matching Expenses with Revenue accounting concept. (p. 515)	7. *T*
8. The percentage of total sales on account method of estimating uncollectible accounts expense assumes that a portion of every sales dollar will become uncollectible. (p. 516)	8. *F*
9. The adjusting entry for Uncollectible Accounts Expense is recorded at the beginning of every accounting period. (p. 516)	9. *F*
10. The adjustment for uncollectible accounts is planned on the work sheet and then recorded in the general journal. (p. 517)	10. *T*
11. The adjusting entry for uncollectible accounts does not affect the balance of the accounts receivable account. (p. 517)	11. *T*
12. When an adjusting entry for uncollectible accounts expense is recorded, Allowance for Uncollectible Accounts is credited. (p. 517)	12. *T*
13. The debit balance of the Uncollectible Accounts Expense account is the estimated uncollectible accounts from sales on account during the next fiscal year. (p. 517)	13. *F*
14. When an account is determined to be uncollectible, a journal entry is made to cancel the uncollectible account. (p. 519)	14. *T*
15. Canceling the balance of a customer account because the customer does not pay is called writing off an account. (p. 519)	15. *T*
16. Allowance for Uncollectible Accounts is debited to write off a customer account. (p. 519)	16. *T*
17. Accounts Receivable is debited to write off a customer account. (p. 519)	17. *F*
18. When a customer account is written off under the allowance method, book value of accounts receivable decreases. (p. 519)	18. *F*
19. Two journal entries are recorded for the collection of a written-off accounts receivable. (p. 521)	19. *T*
20. When a previously written-off account is collected, Accounts Receivable is both debited and credited for the amount collected. (p. 523)	20. *T*

Part Two—Analyzing Uncollectible Accounts Receivable

Directions: For each of the following items, select the choice that best completes the statement. Print the letter identifying your choice in the Answers column.

		Answers
1.	The loss from an uncollectible account is (A) a liability (B) an expense (C) an asset (D) a reduction in revenue (p. 515)	1. *B*
2.	When the percentage of total sales on account method is used, the estimated uncollectible accounts expense is calculated by (A) multiplying total sales on account times the percentage (B) dividing total sales on account by the percentage (C) multiplying total sales times the percentage (D) dividing total sales by the percentage (p. 515)	2. *A*
3.	An Allowance for Uncollectible Accounts balance in the Trial Balance Credit column of a work sheet means (A) there are no uncollectible accounts (B) the estimate has not yet been recorded (C) previous fiscal period estimates have not yet been identified as uncollectible (D) equity has been maintained (p. 516)	3. *C*
4.	At the end of a fiscal period, the account debited to show the estimated amount of uncollectible accounts is (A) Accounts Receivable (B) Cash (C) Uncollectible Accounts Expense (D) Allowance for Uncollectible Accounts (p. 516)	4. *C*
5.	At the end of a fiscal period, the account credited to show the estimated amount of uncollectible accounts is (A) Cash (B) Uncollectible Accounts Expense (C) Accounts Receivable (D) Allowance for Uncollectible Accounts (p. 516)	5. *D*
6.	When the allowance account in the Trial Balance column of a work sheet has a credit balance, the amount of the adjustment is (A) deducted from the trial balance amount (B) not recorded (C) estimated (D) added to the Trial Balance amount (p. 516)	6. *D*
7.	When the account Allowance for Uncollectible Accounts is used, a customer past-due account is written off as uncollectible by (A) debiting Uncollectible Accounts Expense and crediting Accounts Receivable and the customer account (B) debiting Allowance for Uncollectible Accounts and crediting Accounts Receivable and the customer account (C) debiting Accounts Receivable and the customer account and crediting Allowance for Uncollectible Accounts (D) none of these (pp. 519, 520)	7. *B*
8.	To reopen an account previously written off, (A) one general journal entry is recorded (B) two general journal entries are recorded (C) no journal entries are recorded (D) one general journal entry and one cash receipts journal entry are recorded (p. 521)	8. *D*

Name ______________________ Date ______________ Class ______________

Part Three—Journalizing Adjustments for Uncollectible Accounts Expense

Directions: In Answers Column 1, print the abbreviation for the journal in which each transaction is to be recorded. In Answers Columns 2 and 3, print the letters identifying the accounts to be debited and credited for each transaction.

G—General journal CR—Cash receipts journal

Account Titles	Transactions	Answers Journal	Answers Debit	Answers Credit
A. Accounts Receivable	**1–2–3.** Recorded adjusting entry for uncollectible accounts expense. (p. 517)	1. *G*	2. *E*	3. *B*
B. Allowance for Uncollectible Accounts	**4–5–6.** Wrote off Annie's Place past-due account as uncollectible. (pp. 519–520)	4. *G*	5. *B*	6. *A, D*
C. Cash	Received cash in full payment of Annie's Place account, previously written off as uncollectible.			
D. Annie's Place	**7–8–9.** First entry. (p. 521)	7. *G*	8. *A, D*	9. *B*
E. Uncollectible Accounts Expense	**10–11–12.** Second entry. (pp. 522, 523)	10. *CR*	11. *C*	12. *A, D*

Study Skills

Participating in Class Discussions

Have you ever been in a class in which one student monopolized the entire class period? Have you ever been in a class in which one student never said a word? Most of us have. Neither the student who speaks too much nor the student who speaks too little is participating in classroom discussion correctly.

No Time for Shallow Opinions

Some students believe that a class discussion is just a time to express personal opinions. However, class discussions should not be occasions where you speak without thinking. No one is interested in hearing a shallow comment or a long discourse that has not been planned.

Prepare Properly

If you know that a discussion will be held during a certain class period, do everything possible to prepare yourself properly. Read the text assignment thoroughly first. Then read any related material that you can find, particularly items in current newspapers and magazines.

Organize your thoughts so that you will be able to express your ideas in a logical manner. When you have thought through the topic thoroughly, you should practice what you will say a time or two. You should then be able to make a convincing argument during the discussion.

Waiting to Speak

In a class discussion, you should spend a great deal more time listening than speaking. If there are 20 students participating in a large discussion group, you probably should speak a total of no more than one or two minutes. If there are only a few students in the group, you may speak a total of five or six minutes.

As you wait your turn to speak, listen carefully to the opinions of others. Many students do not really pay attention to the ideas of others; they simply wait for the other person to stop speaking so that they may begin. If all ideas are not given serious consideration by all participants in the class, little is gained from a class discussion. There is an old saying that bears repeating: "Keep your ears open; you might learn something."

Presenting Your Ideas

When you have the opportunity to speak in class, present your ideas in a logical order, draw your conclusions, and then stop. You may clarify and illustrate points, but little is gained by simple repetition. Later, if you have other ideas that support your viewpoint, you may express them, following the same guidelines. If you gain the floor just to repeat the points you made previously, you will bore the members of the class, and you will actually hurt your chance of convincing them that you are right.

A Group Effort

Class discussions are excellent ways to learn material. Everyone can share knowledge, and everyone will profit. Prepare properly, listen attentively, and make your points logically. Your opinion will be valued, and you will learn.

Name ____________ Date ________ Class ________

17-1 WORK TOGETHER, p. 518

Estimating and journalizing entries for uncollectible accounts expense

1.

Velson Company
Work Sheet
For Year Ended December 31, 20 – –

	Account Title	1 Trial Balance Debit	2 Trial Balance Credit	3 Adjustments Debit	4 Adjustments Credit
6	Accounts Receivable	867,680.00			
7	Allowance for Uncollectible Accounts		853.00		(e) 6,456.00
47	Uncollectible Accounts Expense			(e) 6,456.00	

2., 3.

GENERAL JOURNAL — PAGE 13

	Date		Account Title	Doc. No.	Post. Ref.	Debit	Credit	
3		31	*Uncollectible Accounts Expense*		*6165*	*6,456.00*		3
4			*Allowance for Uncollectible Accounts*		*1135*		*6,456.00*	4
5								5

3. **GENERAL LEDGER**

ACCOUNT Accounts Receivable — ACCOUNT NO. 1130

Date		Item	Post. Ref.	Debit	Credit	Balance Debit	Balance Credit
20-- Dec.	31	Balance	✔			867,680.00	

ACCOUNT Allowance for Uncollectible Accounts — ACCOUNT NO. 1135

Date		Item	Post. Ref.	Debit	Credit	Balance Debit	Balance Credit
20-- Dec.	31	Balance	✔				853.00
	31		*G13*		*6,456.00*		*7,309.00*

ACCOUNT Uncollectible Accounts Expense — ACCOUNT NO. 6165

Date		Item	Post. Ref.	Debit	Credit	Balance Debit	Balance Credit
20-- *Dec.*	*31*		*G13*	*6,456.00*		*6,456.00*	

17-1 ON YOUR OWN, p. 518

Estimating and journalizing entries for uncollectible accounts expense

1.

McCaffery Industries
Work Sheet
For Year Ended December 31, 20 – –

	ACCOUNT TITLE	1 TRIAL BALANCE DEBIT	2 TRIAL BALANCE CREDIT	3 ADJUSTMENTS DEBIT	4 ADJUSTMENTS CREDIT
6	Accounts Receivable	131,848.50			
7	Allowance for Uncollectible Accounts		216.00		(e) 6,192.20
47	Uncollectible Accounts Expense			(e) 6,192.20	

2., 3.

GENERAL JOURNAL PAGE 26

	DATE		ACCOUNT TITLE	DOC. NO.	POST. REF.	DEBIT	CREDIT	
3		31	*Uncollectible Accounts Expense*		*6165*	*6,192.20*		3
4			*Allowance for Uncollectible Accounts*		*1135*		*6,192.20*	4
5								5

3.

GENERAL LEDGER

ACCOUNT Accounts Receivable — ACCOUNT NO. 1130

DATE		ITEM	POST. REF.	DEBIT	CREDIT	BALANCE DEBIT	BALANCE CREDIT
20-- Dec.	31	Balance	✔			131,848.50	

ACCOUNT Allowance for Uncollectible Accounts — ACCOUNT NO. 1135

DATE		ITEM	POST. REF.	DEBIT	CREDIT	BALANCE DEBIT	BALANCE CREDIT
20-- Dec.	31	Balance	✔				216.00
	31		*G26*		*6,192.20*		*6,408.20*

ACCOUNT Uncollectible Accounts Expense — ACCOUNT NO. 6165

DATE		ITEM	POST. REF.	DEBIT	CREDIT	BALANCE DEBIT	BALANCE CREDIT
20-- Dec.	*31*		*G26*	*6,192.20*		*6,192.20*	

Name ______________ Date ______________ Class ______________

17-2 WORK TOGETHER, p. 524

Recording entries related to uncollectible accounts receivable

1., 2., 3.

GENERAL JOURNAL — PAGE 15

	DATE		ACCOUNT TITLE	DOC. NO.	POST. REF.	DEBIT	CREDIT	
1	20-- Nov.	2	Allowance for Uncollectible Accounts	M245	1130	849 00		1
2			Accounts Receivable/Davidson Corp.		1125/110		849 00	2
3		3	Allowance for Uncollectible Accounts	M247	1130	2,488 00		3
4			Accounts Receivable/JGF Industries		1125/120		2,488 00	4
5		4	Allowance for Uncollectible Accounts	M251	1130	609 00		5
6			Accounts Receivable/Sansing Co.		1125/140		609 00	6
7		14	Accounts Receivable/Lynchburg Co.	M258	1125/130	1,548 00		7
8			Allowance for Uncollectible Accounts		1130		1,548 00	8
9		29	Accounts Receivable/JGF Industries	M261	1125/120	2,488 00		9
10			Allowance for Uncollectible Accounts		1130		2,488 00	10
11								11
12								12

1., 2.

CASH RECEIPTS JOURNAL — PAGE 24

	DATE		ACCOUNT TITLE	DOC. NO.	POST. REF.	1 GENERAL DEBIT	2 GENERAL CREDIT	3 ACCOUNTS RECEIVABLE CREDIT	4 SALES CREDIT	5 SALES TAX PAYABLE CREDIT	6 SALES DISCOUNT DEBIT	7 CASH DEBIT	
1	20-- Nov.	14	Lynchburg Co.	R415	130			1,548 00				1,548 00	1
2		29	JGF Industries	R429	120			2,488 00				2,488 00	2
3													3
4													4
5													5

17-2 WORK TOGETHER (continued)

2.

ACCOUNTS RECEIVABLE LEDGER

CUSTOMER Davidson Corp. CUSTOMER NO. 110

DATE		ITEM	POST. REF.	DEBIT	CREDIT	DEBIT BALANCE
20-- Jan.	9		S1	849 00		849 00
Nov.	2	Written off	G15		849 00	—

CUSTOMER JGF Industries CUSTOMER NO. 120

DATE		ITEM	POST. REF.	DEBIT	CREDIT	DEBIT BALANCE
20-- Mar.	13		S4	2488 00		2488 00
Nov.	3	Written off	G15		2488 00	—
	29	Reopen account	G15	2488 00		2488 00
	29		CR24		2488 00	—

CUSTOMER Lynchburg Co. CUSTOMER NO. 130

DATE		ITEM	POST. REF.	DEBIT	CREDIT	DEBIT BALANCE
20-- Apr.	23	Written off	G5		1548 00	—
Nov.	14	Reopen account	G15	1548 00		1548 00
	14		CR24		1548 00	—

CUSTOMER Sansing Co. CUSTOMER NO. 140

DATE		ITEM	POST. REF.	DEBIT	CREDIT	DEBIT BALANCE
20-- Jan.	22		S2	609 00		609 00
Nov.	4	Written off	G15		609 00	—

17-2 WORK TOGETHER (concluded)

3.

GENERAL LEDGER

ACCOUNT Accounts Receivable — ACCOUNT NO. 1125

DATE		ITEM	POST. REF.	DEBIT	CREDIT	BALANCE DEBIT	BALANCE CREDIT
20-- Nov.	1	Balance	✔			50,148.00	
	2		G15		849.00	49,299.00	
	3		G15		2,488.00	46,811.00	
	4		G15		609.00	46,202.00	
	14		G15	1,548.00		47,750.00	
	29		G15	2,488.00		50,238.00	

ACCOUNT Allowance for Uncollectible Accounts — ACCOUNT NO. 1130

DATE		ITEM	POST. REF.	DEBIT	CREDIT	BALANCE DEBIT	BALANCE CREDIT
20-- Nov.	1	Balance	✔				4,958.00
	2		G15	849.00			4,109.00
	3		G15	2,488.00			1,621.00
	4		G15	609.00			1,012.00
	14		G15		1,548.00		2,560.00
	29		G15		2,488.00		5,048.00

Recording entries related to uncollectible accounts receivable

1., 2., 3.

GENERAL JOURNAL — PAGE 11

	DATE		ACCOUNT TITLE	DOC. NO.	POST. REF.	DEBIT	CREDIT	
1	20-- Oct.	5	Allowance for Uncollectible Accounts	M45	1130	159 00		1
2			Accounts Receivable/Angela White		1125/140		159 00	2
3		8	Allowance for Uncollectible Accounts	M47	1130	612 00		3
4			Accounts Receivable/Peter Ewing		1125/110		612 00	4
5		12	Accounts Receivable/Mike Novak	M51	1125/130	853 00		5
6			Allowance for Uncollectible Accounts		1130		853 00	6
7		16	Allowance for Uncollectible Accounts	M58	1130	238 00		7
8			Accounts Receivable/Tim Haley		1125/120		238 00	8
9		23	Accounts Receivable/Peter Ewing	M61	1125/110	612 00		9
10			Allowance for Uncollectible Accounts		1130		612 00	10
11								11
12								12

1., 2.

CASH RECEIPTS JOURNAL — PAGE 15

	DATE		ACCOUNT TITLE	DOC. NO.	POST. REF.	1 GENERAL DEBIT	2 GENERAL CREDIT	3 ACCOUNTS RECEIVABLE CREDIT	4 SALES CREDIT	5 SALES TAX PAYABLE CREDIT	6 SALES DISCOUNT DEBIT	7 CASH DEBIT	
1	20-- Oct.	12	Mike Novak	R313	130			853 00				853 00	1
2		23	Peter Ewing	R345	110			612 00				612 00	2
3													3
4													4
5													5

Name ______________________ Date ____________ Class ____________

17-2 ON YOUR OWN (continued)

2.

ACCOUNTS RECEIVABLE LEDGER

CUSTOMER Peter Ewing　　　　CUSTOMER NO. 110

DATE		ITEM	POST. REF.	DEBIT	CREDIT	DEBIT BALANCE
20-- Jan.	9		S1	612 00		612 00
Oct.	8	Written off	G11		612 00	—
	23	Reopen account	G11	612 00		612 00
	23		CR15		612 00	—

CUSTOMER Tim Haley　　　　CUSTOMER NO. 120

DATE		ITEM	POST. REF.	DEBIT	CREDIT	DEBIT BALANCE
20-- Mar.	13		S3	238 00		238 00
Oct.	16	Written off	G11		238 00	—

CUSTOMER Mike Novak　　　　CUSTOMER NO. 130

DATE		ITEM	POST. REF.	DEBIT	CREDIT	DEBIT BALANCE
20-- Apr.	6	Written off	G4		853 00	—
Oct.	12	Reopen account	G11	853 00		853 00
	12		CR15		853 00	—

CUSTOMER Angela White　　　　CUSTOMER NO. 140

DATE		ITEM	POST. REF.	DEBIT	CREDIT	DEBIT BALANCE
20-- Feb.	23		S2	159 00		159 00
Oct.	5	Written off	G11		159 00	—

3.

GENERAL LEDGER

ACCOUNT Accounts Receivable — ACCOUNT NO. 1125

DATE		ITEM	POST. REF.	DEBIT	CREDIT	BALANCE DEBIT	BALANCE CREDIT
20-- Oct.	1	Balance	✔			50,148.00	
	5		G11		159.00	49,989.00	
	8		G11		612.00	49,377.00	
	12		G11	853.00		50,230.00	
	16		G11		238.00	49,992.00	
	23		G11	612.00		50,604.00	

ACCOUNT Allowance for Uncollectible Accounts — ACCOUNT NO. 1130

DATE		ITEM	POST. REF.	DEBIT	CREDIT	BALANCE DEBIT	BALANCE CREDIT
20-- Oct.	1	Balance	✔				3,458.00
	5		G11	159.00			3,299.00
	8		G11	612.00			2,687.00
	12		G11		853.00		3,540.00
	16		G11	238.00			3,302.00
	23		G11		612.00		3,914.00

Name ______________________ Date ______________ Class ______________

17-1 APPLICATION PROBLEM, p. 526

Estimating and journalizing entries for uncollectible accounts expense

1.

Kellogg, Inc.

Work Sheet

For Year Ended December 31, 20 – –

	Account Title	Trial Balance Debit (1)	Trial Balance Credit (2)	Adjustments Debit (3)	Adjustments Credit (4)
6	Accounts Receivable	125,848.33			
7	Allowance for Uncollectible Accounts		534.00		(e) *34,260.00*
47	Uncollectible Accounts Expense			(e) *34,260.00*	

2., 3.

GENERAL JOURNAL PAGE 25

	Date		Account Title	Doc. No.	Post. Ref.	Debit	Credit	
3		*31*	*Uncollectible Accounts Expense*		*6165*	*34,260.00*		3
4			*Allowance for Uncollectible Accounts*		*1130*		*34,260.00*	4
5								5

3. **GENERAL LEDGER**

ACCOUNT Accounts Receivable ACCOUNT NO. 1125

Date		Item	Post. Ref.	Debit	Credit	Balance Debit	Balance Credit
20-- Dec.	31	Balance	✔			125,848.33	

ACCOUNT Allowance for Uncollectible Accounts ACCOUNT NO. 1130

Date		Item	Post. Ref.	Debit	Credit	Balance Debit	Balance Credit
20-- Dec.	31	Balance	✔				534.00
	31		*G25*		*34,260.00*		*34,794.00*

ACCOUNT Uncollectible Accounts Expense ACCOUNT NO. 6165

Date		Item	Post. Ref.	Debit	Credit	Balance Debit	Balance Credit
20-- *Dec.*	*31*		*G25*	*34,260.00*		*34,260.00*	

17-2 APPLICATION PROBLEM, p. 526

Recording entries related to uncollectible accounts receivable

1., 2., 3.

GENERAL JOURNAL — PAGE 14

	DATE		ACCOUNT TITLE	DOC. NO.	POST. REF.	DEBIT	CREDIT	
1	20-- Sept.	5	Allowance for Uncollectible Accounts	M234	1130	124 00		1
2			Accounts Receivable/Jackson Company		1125/120		124 00	2
3		7	Accounts Receivable/Davis Industries	M235	1125/110	185 00		3
4			Allowance for Uncollectible Accounts		1130		185 00	4
5		14	Allowance for Uncollectible Accounts	M238	1130	215 00		5
6			Accounts Receivable/Lancing, Inc.		1125/130		215 00	6
7		19	Allowance for Uncollectible Accounts	M243	1130	842 00		7
8			Accounts Receivable/Sanders Mfg.		1125/140		842 00	8
9		27	Accounts Receivable/Jackson Company	M251	1125/120	124 00		9
10			Allowance for Uncollectible Accounts		1130		124 00	10
11								11
12								12

1., 2.

CASH RECEIPTS JOURNAL — PAGE 19

	DATE		ACCOUNT TITLE	DOC. NO.	POST. REF.	1 GENERAL DEBIT	2 GENERAL CREDIT	3 ACCOUNTS RECEIVABLE CREDIT	4 SALES CREDIT	5 SALES TAX PAYABLE CREDIT	6 SALES DISCOUNT DEBIT	7 CASH DEBIT	
1	20-- Sept.	7	Davis Industries	R339	110			185 00				185 00	1
2		27	Jackson Company	R362	120			124 00				124 00	2
3													3
4													4
5													5

17-2 APPLICATION PROBLEM (continued)

2.

ACCOUNTS RECEIVABLE LEDGER

CUSTOMER Davis Industries — CUSTOMER NO. 110

DATE		ITEM	POST. REF.	DEBIT	CREDIT	DEBIT BALANCE
20-- Feb.	23	Written off	G2		185 00	—
Sept.	7	Reopen account	G14	185 00		185 00
	7		CR19		185 00	—

CUSTOMER Jackson Company — CUSTOMER NO. 120

DATE		ITEM	POST. REF.	DEBIT	CREDIT	DEBIT BALANCE
20-- Jan.	4		S1	124 00		124 00
Sept.	5	Written off	G14		124 00	—
	27	Reopen account	G14	124 00		124 00
	27		CR19		124 00	—

CUSTOMER Lancing, Inc. — CUSTOMER NO. 130

DATE		ITEM	POST. REF.	DEBIT	CREDIT	DEBIT BALANCE
20-- Apr.	2		S7	215 00		215 00
Sept.	14	Written off	G14		215 00	—

CUSTOMER Sanders Mfg. — CUSTOMER NO. 140

DATE		ITEM	POST. REF.	DEBIT	CREDIT	DEBIT BALANCE
20-- Jan.	23		S2	842 00		842 00
Sept.	19	Written off	G14		842 00	—

3.

GENERAL LEDGER

ACCOUNT Accounts Receivable — ACCOUNT NO. 1125

DATE		ITEM	POST. REF.	DEBIT	CREDIT	BALANCE DEBIT	BALANCE CREDIT
20-- Sept.	1	Balance	✔			23 484 00	
	5		G14		124 00	23 360 00	
	7		G14	185 00		23 545 00	
	14		G14		215 00	23 330 00	
	19		G14		842 00	22 488 00	
	27		G14	124 00		22 612 00	

ACCOUNT Allowance for Uncollectible Accounts — ACCOUNT NO. 1130

DATE		ITEM	POST. REF.	DEBIT	CREDIT	BALANCE DEBIT	BALANCE CREDIT
20-- Sept.	1	Balance	✔				2 448 00
	5		G14	124 00			2 324 00
	7		G14		185 00		2 509 00
	14		G14	215 00			2 294 00
	19		G14	842 00			1 452 00
	27		G14		124 00		1 576 00

Name ____________________ Date ____________ Class ____________

17-3 APPLICATION PROBLEM, p. 527

Recording entries related to uncollectible accounts receivable

1., 2., 3.

GENERAL JOURNAL — PAGE 4

	DATE		ACCOUNT TITLE	DOC. NO.	POST. REF.	DEBIT	CREDIT	
1	20-- Feb.	3	Accounts Receivable/Bearden Co.	M24	1130/110	1458 00		1
2			Allowance for Uncollectible Accounts		1135		1458 00	2
3		7	Allowance for Uncollectible Accounts	M25	1135	2584 00		3
4			Accounts Receivable/Hampton Industries		1130/130		2584 00	4
5		10	Allowance for Uncollectible Accounts	M28	1135	948 00		5
6			Accounts Receivable/Rankin Co.		1130/140		948 00	6
7		12	Accounts Receivable/Camden Enterprises	M31	1130/120	1784 00		7
8			Allowance for Uncollectible Accounts		1135		1784 00	8
9		21	Allowance for Uncollectible Accounts	M34	1135	548 00		9
10			Accounts Receivable/Wilmont Co.		1130/150		548 00	10
11		27	Accounts Receivable/Hampton Industries	M35	1130/130	2584 00		11
12			Allowance for Uncollectible Accounts		1135		2584 00	12
13								13
14								14

1., 2.

CASH RECEIPTS JOURNAL — PAGE 2

	DATE		ACCOUNT TITLE	DOC. NO.	POST. REF.	1 GENERAL DEBIT	2 GENERAL CREDIT	3 ACCOUNTS RECEIVABLE CREDIT	4 SALES CREDIT	5 SALES TAX PAYABLE CREDIT	6 SALES DISCOUNT DEBIT	7 CASH DEBIT	
1	20-- Feb.	3	Bearden Co.	R134	110			1458 00				1458 00	1
2		12	Camden Enterprises	R142	120			1784 00				1784 00	2
3		27	Hampton Industries	R159	130			2584 00				2584 00	3
4													4
5													5

2.

ACCOUNTS RECEIVABLE LEDGER

CUSTOMER Bearden Co. — CUSTOMER NO. 110

DATE		ITEM	POST. REF.	DEBIT	CREDIT	DEBIT BALANCE
20-- Jan.	3	Written off	G1		1 458 00	—
Feb.	3	Reopen account	G4	1 458 00		1 458 00
	3		CR2		1 458 00	—

CUSTOMER Camden Enterprises — CUSTOMER NO. 120

DATE		ITEM	POST. REF.	DEBIT	CREDIT	DEBIT BALANCE
20-- Jan.	3	Written off	G1		1 784 00	—
Feb.	12	Reopen account	G4	1 784 00		1 784 00
	12		CR2		1 784 00	—

CUSTOMER Hampton Industries — CUSTOMER NO. 130

DATE		ITEM	POST. REF.	DEBIT	CREDIT	DEBIT BALANCE
20-- Jan.	1	Balance	✔			2 584 00
Feb.	7	Written off	G4		2 584 00	—
	27	Reopen account	G4	2 584 00		2 584 00
	27		CR2		2 584 00	—

CUSTOMER Rankin Co. — CUSTOMER NO. 140

DATE		ITEM	POST. REF.	DEBIT	CREDIT	DEBIT BALANCE
20-- Jan.	1	Balance	✔			948 00
Feb.	10	Written off	G4		948 00	—

CUSTOMER Wilmont Co. — CUSTOMER NO. 150

DATE		ITEM	POST. REF.	DEBIT	CREDIT	DEBIT BALANCE
20-- Jan.	1	Balance	✔			548 00
Feb.	21	Written off	G4		548 00	—

17-3 APPLICATION PROBLEM (concluded)

3.

GENERAL LEDGER

ACCOUNT Accounts Receivable — ACCOUNT NO. 1130

DATE		ITEM	POST. REF.	DEBIT	CREDIT	BALANCE DEBIT	BALANCE CREDIT
20-- Feb.	1	Balance	✔			54 158 00	
	3		G4	1 458 00		55 616 00	
	7		G4		2 584 00	53 032 00	
	10		G4		948 00	52 084 00	
	12		G4	1 784 00		53 868 00	
	21		G4		548 00	53 320 00	
	27		G4	2 584 00		55 904 00	

ACCOUNT Allowance for Uncollectible Accounts — ACCOUNT NO. 1135

DATE		ITEM	POST. REF.	DEBIT	CREDIT	BALANCE DEBIT	BALANCE CREDIT
20-- Feb.	1	Balance	✔				2 514 00
	3		G4		1 458 00		3 972 00
	7		G4	2 584 00			1 388 00
	10		G4	948 00			440 00
	12		G4		1 784 00		2 224 00
	21		G4	548 00			1 676 00
	27		G4		2 584 00		4 260 00

17-4 MASTERY PROBLEM, p. 527

Recording entries for uncollectible accounts

1.

GENERAL JOURNAL PAGE 20

	DATE		ACCOUNT TITLE	DOC. NO.	POST. REF.	DEBIT	CREDIT	
1	20-- Oct.	8	Allowance for Uncollectible Accounts	M243	1130	648 25		1
2			Accounts Receivable/Keller Corporation		1125/140		648 25	2
3		19	Allowance for Uncollectible Accounts	M252	1130	948 00		3
4			Accounts Receivable/Gason Company		1125/130		948 00	4
5								5

2.

GENERAL JOURNAL PAGE 22

	DATE		ACCOUNT TITLE	DOC. NO.	POST. REF.	DEBIT	CREDIT	
1	20-- Nov.	9	Allowance for Uncollectible Accounts	M267	1130	815 00		1
2			Accounts Receivable/Baker Co.		1125/110		815 00	2
3		18	Accounts Receivable/Keller Corporation	M274	1125/140	648 25		3
4			Allowance for Uncollectible Accounts		1130		648 25	4
5		23	Accounts Receivable/Pearson Industries	M281	1125/150	251 80		5
6			Allowance for Uncollectible Accounts		1130		251 80	6

3.

GENERAL JOURNAL PAGE 24

	DATE		ACCOUNT TITLE	DOC. NO.	POST. REF.	DEBIT	CREDIT	
1	20-- Dec.	4	Allowance for Uncollectible Accounts	M291	1130	1 458 00		1
2			Accounts Receivable/Franklin, Inc.		1125/120		1 458 00	2
3		10	Accounts Receivable/Baker Corp.	M293	1125/110	815 00		3
4			Allowance for Uncollectible Accounts		1130		815 00	4
5		29	Accounts Receivable/Gason Company	M297	1125/130	948 00		5
6			Allowance for Uncollectible Accounts		1130		948 00	6

4.

GENERAL JOURNAL PAGE 26

	DATE		ACCOUNT TITLE	DOC. NO.	POST. REF.	DEBIT	CREDIT	
1			Adjusting Entries					1
2	20-- Dec.	31	Uncollectible Accounts Expense		6165	8 274 00		2
3			Allowance for Uncollectible Accounts		1130		8 274 00	3
4								4
5								5

Name ______________________ Date ____________ Class ____________

17-4 MASTERY PROBLEM (continued)

2.

CASH RECEIPTS JOURNAL — PAGE 24

	DATE		ACCOUNT TITLE	DOC. NO.	POST. REF.	GENERAL DEBIT (1)	GENERAL CREDIT (2)	ACCOUNTS RECEIVABLE CREDIT (3)	SALES CREDIT (4)	SALES TAX PAYABLE CREDIT (5)	SALES DISCOUNT DEBIT (6)	CASH DEBIT (7)	
1	20-- Nov.	18	Keller Corporation	R453	140			648 25				648 25	1
2		23	Pearson Industries	R476	150			251 80				251 80	2
3		30	Totals					900 05				900 05	3
4								(1125)					4
5													5

3.

CASH RECEIPTS JOURNAL — PAGE 26

	DATE		ACCOUNT TITLE	DOC. NO.	POST. REF.	GENERAL DEBIT (1)	GENERAL CREDIT (2)	ACCOUNTS RECEIVABLE CREDIT (3)	SALES CREDIT (4)	SALES TAX PAYABLE CREDIT (5)	SALES DISCOUNT DEBIT (6)	CASH DEBIT (7)	
1	20-- Dec.	10	Baker Corp.	R489	110			815 00				815 00	1
2		29	Gason Company	R502	130			948 00				948 00	2
3		31	Totals					1 763 00				1 763 00	3
4								(1125)					4
5													5

17-4 MASTERY PROBLEM (continued)

1., 2., 3.

ACCOUNTS RECEIVABLE LEDGER

CUSTOMER Baker Corp. — CUSTOMER NO. 110

DATE		ITEM	POST. REF.	DEBIT	CREDIT	DEBIT BALANCE
20-- Feb.	11		S4	815 00		815 00
Nov.	*9*	*Written off*	*G22*		*815 00*	—
Dec.	*10*	*Reopen account*	*G24*	*815 00*		*815 00*
	10		*CR26*		*815 00*	—

CUSTOMER Franklin, Inc. — CUSTOMER NO. 120

DATE		ITEM	POST. REF.	DEBIT	CREDIT	DEBIT BALANCE
20-- Mar.	15		S5	1 458 00		1 458 00
Dec.	*4*	*Written off*	*G24*		*1 458 00*	—

CUSTOMER Gason Company — CUSTOMER NO. 130

DATE		ITEM	POST. REF.	DEBIT	CREDIT	DEBIT BALANCE
20-- Jan.	1	Balance	✔			948 00
Oct.	*19*	*Written off*	*G20*		*948 00*	—
Dec.	*29*	*Reopen account*	*G24*	*948 00*		*948 00*
	29		*CR26*		*948 00*	—

CUSTOMER Keller Corporation — CUSTOMER NO. 140

DATE		ITEM	POST. REF.	DEBIT	CREDIT	DEBIT BALANCE
20-- Jan.	1	Balance	✔			648 25
Oct.	*8*	*Written off*	*G20*		*648 25*	—
Nov.	*18*	*Reopen account*	*G22*	*648 25*		*648 25*
	18		*CR24*		*648 25*	—

CUSTOMER Pearson Industries — CUSTOMER NO. 150

DATE		ITEM	POST. REF.	DEBIT	CREDIT	DEBIT BALANCE
20-- Apr.	14	Written off	G8		251 80	—
Nov.	*23*	*Reopen account*	*G22*	*251 80*		*251 80*
	23		*CR24*		*251 80*	—

Name ______________________ Date ______________ Class ______________

17-4 MASTERY PROBLEM (concluded)

1., 2., 3., 4.

GENERAL LEDGER

ACCOUNT Accounts Receivable — ACCOUNT NO. 1125

DATE		ITEM	POST. REF.	DEBIT	CREDIT	BALANCE DEBIT	BALANCE CREDIT
20-- Oct.	1	Balance	✔			68,452.30	
	8		G20		648.25	67,804.05	
	19		G20		948.00	66,856.05	
Nov.	9		G22		815.00	66,041.05	
	18		G22	648.25		66,689.30	
	23		G22	251.80		66,941.10	
	30		CR24		900.05	66,041.05	
Dec.	4		G24		1,458.00	64,583.05	
	10		G24	815.00		65,398.05	
	29		G24	948.00		66,346.05	
	31		CR26		1,763.00	64,583.05	

ACCOUNT Allowance for Uncollectible Accounts — ACCOUNT NO. 1130

DATE		ITEM	POST. REF.	DEBIT	CREDIT	BALANCE DEBIT	BALANCE CREDIT
20-- Oct.	1	Balance	✔				3,210.00
	8		G20	648.25			2,561.75
	19		G20	948.00			1,613.75
Nov.	9		G22	815.00			798.75
	18		G22		648.25		1,447.00
	23		G22		251.80		1,698.80
Dec.	4		G24	1,458.00			240.80
	10		G24		815.00		1,055.80
	29		G24		948.00		2,003.80
	31		G26		8,274.00		10,277.80

ACCOUNT Uncollectible Accounts Expense — ACCOUNT NO. 6165

DATE		ITEM	POST. REF.	DEBIT	CREDIT	BALANCE DEBIT	BALANCE CREDIT
20-- Dec.	31		G26	8,274.00		8,274.00	

17-5 CHALLENGE PROBLEM, p. 528

Recording entries for uncollectible accounts

During the past five years, the company's addition to Allowance for Uncollectible Accounts appears to have no connection to its steady growth of sales or actual uncollectible accounts. The charge to Uncollectible Accounts Expense for two years was $8,000, then increased to $15,000 for three years. These annual charges have varied from 1.14% to 1.76% of sales on account.

The five-year total of actual accounts written off, net of the accounts collected after being written off, was $66,000. This amount is 1.51% of total sales on account of $4,375,000. Using a rounded percentage of 1.5%, the company should charge $21,000 of expected sales $1,400,000.

Study Guide 18	**Name**	**Perfect Score**	**Your Score**
	Identifying Accounting Terms	7 Pts.	
	Analyzing Plant Asset Transactions	14 Pts.	
	Analyzing Plant Assets and Depreciation	10 Pts.	
	Total	31 Pts.	

Part One—Identifying Accounting Terms

Directions: Select the one term in Column I that best fits each definition in Column II. Print the letter identifying your choice in the Answers column.

Column I	***Column II***	***Answers***
A. assessed value	**1.** Land and anything attached to the land. (p. 536)	**1.** *G*
B. declining-balance method of depreciation	**2.** All property not classified as real property. (p. 536)	**2.** *E*
C. gain on plant assets	**3.** The value of an asset determined by tax authorities for the purpose of calculating taxes. (p. 536)	**3.** *A*
D. loss on plant assets	**4.** An accounting form on which a business records information about each plant asset. (p. 542)	**4.** *F*
E. personal property	**5.** Revenue that results when a plant asset is sold for more than book value. (p. 548)	**5.** *C*
F. plant asset record	**6.** The loss that results when a plant asset is sold for less than book value. (p. 549)	**6.** *D*
G. real property	**7.** Multiplying the book value by a constant depreciation rate at the end of each fiscal period. (p. 551)	**7.** *B*

Part Two—Analyzing Plant Asset Transactions

Directions: Analyze each of the following transactions into debit and credit parts. Print the letter identifying your choices in the proper Answers column.

Account Titles

A. Accumulated Depreciation—Office Equipment
B. Accumulated Depreciation—Store Equipment
C. Cash
D. Depreciation Expense—Office Equipment
E. Depreciation Expense—Store Equipment
F. Gain on Plant Assets
G. Office Equipment
H. Loss on Plant Assets
I. Property Tax Expense
J. Store Equipment

Transactions	Answers Debit	Answers Credit
1–2. Paid cash for new display case. (p. 535)	1. *J*	2. *C*
3–4. Paid cash for property taxes. (p. 536)	3. *I*	4. *C*
5–6. Recorded annual store equipment depreciation. (p. 543)	5. *E*	6. *B*
7–8. Received cash from sale of display case for book value. (p. 546)	7. *B, C*	8. *J*
9–10. Recorded a partial year's depreciation on a cash register to be sold. (p. 547)	9. *E*	10. *B*
11–12. Received cash from sale of cash register for more than book value. (p. 548)	11. *B, C*	12. *F, J*
13–14. Received cash from sale of a computer for less than book value. (p. 549)	13. *A, C, H*	14. *G*

Name ______________________ Date ____________ Class ____________

Part Three—Analyzing Plant Assets and Depreciation

Directions: For each of the following items, select the choice that best completes the statement. Print the letter identifying your choice in the Answers column.

Answers

1. Recording a plant asset at its original cost is an application of the concept (A) Going Concern (B) Matching Expenses with Revenue (C) Objective Evidence (D) Historical Cost (p. 535) — 1. *D*

2. The smallest unit of time used to calculate depreciation is (A) one month (B) half a year (C) one year (D) none of these (p. 539) — 2. *A*

3. The annual depreciation for a plant asset with original cost of $1,000.00, estimated salvage value of $100.00, and estimated useful life of 10 years, using the straight-line method, is (A) $100.00 (B) $1,000.00 (C) $900.00 (D) $90.00 (p. 539) — 3. *D*

4. The accumulated depreciation account should show (A) total depreciation for plant assets since the business was formed (B) total depreciation for plant assets still in use (C) only total depreciation expense for plant assets for the current year (D) next year's estimated depreciation for plant assets (p. 540) — 4. *B*

5. When a plant asset is sold for the asset's book value, (A) cash received plus accumulated depreciation equals original cost (B) cash received plus salvage value equals original cost (C) cash received plus accumulated depreciation plus salvage value equals original cost (D) none of these (p. 546) — 5. *A*

6. When a plant asset is sold for more than the asset's book value, (A) cash received plus accumulated depreciation plus gain on disposal equals original cost plus gain on disposal (B) cash received plus accumulated depreciation equals original cost plus gain on disposal (C) cash received plus accumulated depreciation plus loss on disposal equals original cost (D) cash received plus accumulated depreciation equals original cost plus loss on disposal (p. 548) — 6. *B*

7. When a plant asset is sold for less than the asset's book value, (A) cash received plus accumulated depreciation plus gain on disposal equals original cost (B) cash received plus accumulated depreciation plus loss on disposal equals original cost (C) cash received plus accumulated depreciation equals original cost plus gain on disposal (D) cash received plus accumulated depreciation equals original cost plus loss on disposal (p. 549) — 7. *B*

8. Charging more depreciation expense in the early years is an application of the concept of (A) Matching Expenses with Revenue (B) Realization of Revenue (C) Adequate Disclosure (D) Historical Cost (p. 551) — 8. *A*

9. The declining-balance method of depreciation is calculated by (A) charging an equal amount of depreciation each year (B) subtracting the annual depreciation expense from the book value (C) multiplying the book value by a constant depreciation rate at the end of each fiscal period (D) none of the above (p. 551) — 9. *C*

10. The double declining-balance method of depreciation (A) records a greater depreciation expense in the early years of an asset's useful life (B) records a lesser depreciation expense in the early years of an asset's useful life (C) slows down the recording of depreciation in the early years of an asset's useful life (D) accelerates the recording of depreciation in the later years of an asset's useful life (p. 553) — 10. *A*

Name ______________________ Date ______________ Class ______________

18-1 WORK TOGETHER, p. 537

Journalizing buying plant assets and paying property tax

1., 2.

CASH PAYMENTS JOURNAL — PAGE 1

	DATE		ACCOUNT TITLE	CK. NO.	POST. REF.	1 GENERAL DEBIT	2 GENERAL CREDIT	3 ACCOUNTS PAYABLE DEBIT	4 PURCHASES DISCOUNT CREDIT	5 CASH CREDIT	
1	20-- Jan.	3	*Store Equipment*	142	1215	500 00				500 00	1
2		5	*Office Equipment*	145	1205	400 00				400 00	2
3	Feb.	26	*Property Tax Expense*	182	6145	2,400 00				2,400 00	3
4	July	2	*Office Equipment*	216	1205	260 00				260 00	4

2.

GENERAL LEDGER

ACCOUNT Office Equipment — ACCOUNT NO. 1205

DATE		ITEM	POST. REF.	DEBIT	CREDIT	BALANCE DEBIT	BALANCE CREDIT
20-- Jan.	1	Balance	✓			15,480 00	
	5		CP1	400 00		15,880 00	
July	2		CP1	260 00		16,140 00	

ACCOUNT Store Equipment — ACCOUNT NO. 1215

DATE		ITEM	POST. REF.	DEBIT	CREDIT	BALANCE DEBIT	BALANCE CREDIT
20-- Jan.	1	Balance	✓			9,730 00	
	3		CP1	500 00		10,230 00	

ACCOUNT Property Tax Expense — ACCOUNT NO. 6145

DATE		ITEM	POST. REF.	DEBIT	CREDIT	BALANCE DEBIT	BALANCE CREDIT
20-- Feb.	26		CP1	2,400 00		2,400 00	

Journalizing buying plant assets and paying property tax

1., 2.

CASH PAYMENTS JOURNAL PAGE 1

	DATE		ACCOUNT TITLE	CK. NO.	POST. REF.	1 GENERAL DEBIT	2 GENERAL CREDIT	3 ACCOUNTS PAYABLE DEBIT	4 PURCHASES DISCOUNT CREDIT	5 CASH CREDIT	
1	20-- Jan.	2	Office Equipment	215	1205	1 800 00				1 800 00	1
2		5	Store Equipment	216	1215	520 00				520 00	2
3	Feb.	24	Property Tax Expense	232	6145	1 800 00				1 800 00	3
4	Mar.	13	Store Equipment	283	1215	325 00				325 00	4

2.

GENERAL LEDGER

ACCOUNT Office Equipment ACCOUNT NO. 1205

DATE		ITEM	POST. REF.	DEBIT	CREDIT	BALANCE DEBIT	BALANCE CREDIT
20-- Jan.	1	Balance	✔			15 480 00	
	2		CP1	1 800 00		17 280 00	

ACCOUNT Store Equipment ACCOUNT NO. 1215

DATE		ITEM	POST. REF.	DEBIT	CREDIT	BALANCE DEBIT	BALANCE CREDIT
20-- Jan.	1	Balance	✔			9 730 00	
	5		CP1	520 00		10 250 00	
Mar.	13		CP1	325 00		10 575 00	

ACCOUNT Property Tax Expense ACCOUNT NO. 6145

DATE		ITEM	POST. REF.	DEBIT	CREDIT	BALANCE DEBIT	BALANCE CREDIT
20-- Feb.	24		CP1	1 800 00		1 800 00	

Name ______________________ Date ______________ Class ______________

18-2 WORK TOGETHER, p. 541

Calculating depreciation

Plant asset:	*Computer Monitor*	Original cost:	*$560.00*
Depreciation method:	*Straight-line*	Estimated salvage value:	*$ 60.00*
		Estimated useful life:	*5 years*
		Date bought:	*January 3, 20X1*

Year	Beginning Book Value	Annual Depreciation	Accumulated Depreciation	Ending Book Value
20X1	*$560.00*	*$100.00*	*$100.00*	*$460.00*
20X2	*460.00*	*100.00*	*200.00*	*360.00*
20X3	*360.00*	*100.00*	*300.00*	*260.00*
20X4	*260.00*	*100.00*	*400.00*	*160.00*
20X5	*160.00*	*100.00*	*500.00*	*60.00*

Plant asset:	*Notebook Computer*	Original cost:	*$2,750.00*
Depreciation method:	*Straight-line*	Estimated salvage value:	*$ 350.00*
		Estimated useful life:	*4 years*
		Date bought:	*October 19, 20X1*

Year	Beginning Book Value	Annual Depreciation	Accumulated Depreciation	Ending Book Value
20X1	*$2,750.00*	*$100.00*	*$ 100.00*	*$2,650.00*
20X2	*2,650.00*	*600.00*	*700.00*	*2,050.00*
20X3	*2,050.00*	*600.00*	*1,300.00*	*1,450.00*
20X4	*1,450.00*	*600.00*	*1,900.00*	*850.00*
20X5	*850.00*	*500.00*	*2,400.00*	*350.00*

18-2 ON YOUR OWN, p. 541

Calculating depreciation

Plant asset:	*Sound System*	Original cost:	*$5,600.00*
Depreciation method:	*Straight-line*	Estimated salvage value:	*$ 400.00*
		Estimated useful life:	*8 years*
		Date bought:	*January 6, 20X1*

Year	Beginning Book Value	Annual Depreciation	Accumulated Depreciation	Ending Book Value
20X1	*$5,600.00*	*$650.00*	*$ 650.00*	*$4,950.00*
20X2	*4,950.00*	*650.00*	*1,300.00*	*4,300.00*
20X3	*4,300.00*	*650.00*	*1,950.00*	*3,650.00*
20X4	*3,650.00*	*650.00*	*2,600.00*	*3,000.00*
20X5	*3,000.00*	*650.00*	*3,250.00*	*2,350.00*
20X6	*2,350.00*	*650.00*	*3,900.00*	*1,700.00*
20X7	*1,700.00*	*650.00*	*4,550.00*	*1,050.00*
20X8	*1,050.00*	*650.00*	*5,200.00*	*400.00*

Plant asset:	*Shredder*	Original cost:	*$1,250.00*
Depreciation method:	*Straight-line*	Estimated salvage value:	*$ 50.00*
		Estimated useful life:	*5 years*
		Date bought:	*May 22, 20X1*

Year	Beginning Book Value	Annual Depreciation	Accumulated Depreciation	Ending Book Value
20X1	*$1,250.00*	*$140.00*	*$ 140.00*	*$1,110.00*
20X2	*1,110.00*	*240.00*	*380.00*	*870.00*
20X3	*870.00*	*240.00*	*620.00*	*630.00*
20X4	*630.00*	*240.00*	*860.00*	*390.00*
20X5	*390.00*	*240.00*	*1,100.00*	*150.00*
20X6	*150.00*	*100.00*	*1,200.00*	*50.00*

Name ______________________ Date ____________ Class ____________

18-3 WORK TOGETHER, p. 545

Journalizing depreciation

1.

PLANT ASSET RECORD No. *241*   General Ledger Account No. *1215*

Description *Computer Monitor*   General Ledger Account *Store Equipment*

Date Bought *January 3, 20X1*   Serial Number *51-4882*   Original Cost *$560.00*

Estimated Useful Life *5 years*   Estimated Salvage Value *$60.00*   Depreciation Method *Straight-line*

WT 18-3

Disposed of: Discarded ______ Sold *✔* Traded ______

Date *January 6, 20X4*   Disposal Amount *$290.00*

WT 18-4

Year	Annual Depreciation Expense	Accumulated Depreciation	Ending Book Value
20X1	$100.00	$100.00	$460.00
20X2	100.00	200.00	360.00
20X3	100.00	300.00	260.00

WT 18-3

PLANT ASSET RECORD No. *242*   General Ledger Account No. *1205*

Description *Notebook Computer*   General Ledger Account *Office Equipment*

Date Bought *October 19, 20X1*   Serial Number *GY1281*   Original Cost *$2,750.00*

Estimated Useful Life *4 years*   Estimated Salvage Value *$350.00*   Depreciation Method *Straight-line*

WT 18-3

Disposed of: Discarded ______ Sold *✔* Traded ______

Date *July 12, 20X4*   Disposal Amount *$800.00*

WT 18-4

Year	Annual Depreciation Expense	Accumulated Depreciation	Ending Book Value
20X1	$100.00	$ 100.00	$2,650.00
20X2	600.00	700.00	2,050.00
20X3	600.00	1,300.00	1,450.00
20X4	300.00	1,600.00	1,150.00

WT 18-3 (20X1–20X3); WT 18-4 (20X4)

2.

Fairbrother, Inc.
Work Sheet
For Year Ended December 31, 20 – –

	Account Title	1 Trial Balance Debit	2 Trial Balance Credit	3 Adjustments Debit	4 Adjustments Credit
10	Office Equipment	28 485 25			
11	Accumulated Depreciation—Office Equipment		14 522 00		(f) 4 230 00
38	Depreciation Expense—Office Equipment			(f) 4 230 00	

GENERAL JOURNAL PAGE 20

	Date		Account Title	Doc. No.	Post. Ref.	Debit	Credit	
1			*Adjusting Entries*					1
2	20-- Dec.	31	*Depreciation Expense—Office Equipment*		*6120*	*4 230 00*		2
3			*Accumulated Depreciation—Office Equipment*		*1210*		*4 230 00*	3
4								4
5								5

GENERAL LEDGER

ACCOUNT Office Equipment ACCOUNT NO. 1205

Date		Item	Post. Ref.	Debit	Credit	Balance Debit	Balance Credit
20-- Dec.	31	Balance	✔			28 485 25	

ACCOUNT Accumulated Depreciation—Office Equipment ACCOUNT NO. 1210

Date		Item	Post. Ref.	Debit	Credit	Balance Debit	Balance Credit
20-- Dec.	31	Balance	✔				14 522 00
	31		*G20*		*4 230 00*		*18 752 00*

ACCOUNT Depreciation Expense—Office Equipment ACCOUNT NO. 6120

Date		Item	Post. Ref.	Debit	Credit	Balance Debit	Balance Credit
20-- *Dec.*	*31*		*G20*	*4 230 00*		*4 230 00*	

Name ____________ Date ________ Class ________

18-3 ON YOUR OWN, p. 545

Journalizing depreciation

1.

PLANT ASSET RECORD No. *353* General Ledger Account No. *1215*

Description *Sound System* General Ledger Account *Store Equipment*

Date Bought *January 6, 20X1* Serial Number *12488BF2* Original Cost *$5,600.00*

Estimated Useful Life *8 years* Estimated Salvage Value *$400.00* Depreciation Method *Straight-line*

OYO 18-3

Disposed of: Discarded ______ Sold *✔* Traded ______

Date *January 2, 20X4* Disposal Amount *$4,000.00*

OYO 18-4

Year	Annual Depreciation Expense	Accumulated Depreciation	Ending Book Value
20X1	$650.00	$ 650.00	$4,950.00
20X2	650.00	1,300.00	4,300.00
20X3	650.00	1,950.00	3,650.00

OYO 18-3

PLANT ASSET RECORD No. *354* General Ledger Account No. *1205*

Description *Shredder* General Ledger Account *Office Equipment*

Date Bought *May 22, 20X1* Serial Number *34-432-2* Original Cost *$1,250.00*

Estimated Useful Life *5 years* Estimated Salvage Value *$50.00* Depreciation Method *Straight-line*

OYO 18-3

Disposed of: Discarded ______ Sold *✔* Traded ______

Date *October 3, 20X4* Disposal Amount *$325.00*

OYO 18-4

Year	Annual Depreciation Expense	Accumulated Depreciation	Ending Book Value
20X1	$140.00	$140.00	$1,110.00
20X2	240.00	380.00	870.00
20X3	240.00	620.00	630.00
20X4	180.00	800.00	450.00

OYO 18-3 (20X1–20X3); OYO 18-4 (20X4)

18-3 ON YOUR OWN (concluded)

2.

Wrench Co.
Work Sheet
For Year Ended December 31, 20 – –

	Account Title	Trial Balance Debit (1)	Trial Balance Credit (2)	Adjustments Debit (3)	Adjustments Credit (4)
12	Store Equipment	35 848 22			
13	Accumulated Depreciation—Store Equipment		24 118 00		(g) 9 880 00
39	Depreciation Expense—Store Equipment			(g) 9 880 00	

GENERAL JOURNAL PAGE 18

	Date		Account Title	Doc. No.	Post. Ref.	Debit	Credit	
1			*Adjusting Entries*					1
2	20 – – *Dec.*	*31*	*Depreciation Expense—Store Equipment*		*6125*	*9 880 00*		2
3			*Accumulated Depreciation—Store Equipment*		*1220*		*9 880 00*	3
4								4

GENERAL LEDGER

ACCOUNT Store Equipment ACCOUNT NO. 1215

Date		Item	Post. Ref.	Debit	Credit	Balance Debit	Balance Credit
20 – – Dec.	31	Balance	✔			35 848 22	

ACCOUNT Accumulated Depreciation—Store Equipment ACCOUNT NO. 1220

Date		Item	Post. Ref.	Debit	Credit	Balance Debit	Balance Credit
20 – – Dec.	31	Balance	✔				24 118 00
	31		*G18*		*9 880 00*		*33 998 00*

ACCOUNT Depreciation Expense—Store Equipment ACCOUNT NO. 6125

Date		Item	Post. Ref.	Debit	Credit	Balance Debit	Balance Credit
20 – – *Dec.*	*31*		*G18*	*9 880 00*		*9 880 00*	

18-4 WORK TOGETHER, p. 550

Recording the disposal of plant assets

1.

GENERAL JOURNAL — PAGE 11

	DATE		ACCOUNT TITLE	DOC. NO.	POST. REF.	DEBIT	CREDIT	
1	20-- July	12	Depreciation Expense—Office Equipment	M67		300 00		1
2			Accumulated Depreciation—Office Equipment				300 00	2
3								3
4								4
5								5

2.

CASH RECEIPTS JOURNAL — PAGE 1

	DATE		ACCOUNT TITLE	DOC. NO.	POST. REF.	1 GENERAL DEBIT	2 GENERAL CREDIT	3 ACCOUNTS RECEIVABLE CREDIT	4 SALES CREDIT	5 SALES TAX PAYABLE CREDIT	6 SALES DISCOUNT DEBIT	7 CASH DEBIT	
1	20X4 Jan.	6	Accum. Depr.—Store Equip.	R4		300 00						290 00	1
2			Store Equipment				560 00						2
3			Gain on Plant Assets				30 00						3
4	July	12	Accum. Depr.—Office Equip.	R203		1600 00						800 00	4
5			Loss on Plant Assets			350 00							5
6			Office Equipment				2750 00						6
7													7

Recording the disposal of plant assets

1.

GENERAL JOURNAL

PAGE 10

DATE		ACCOUNT TITLE	DOC. NO.	POST. REF.	DEBIT	CREDIT
20-- Oct.	3	*Depreciation Expense—Office Equipment*	*M82*		180 00	
		Accumulated Depreciation—Office Equipment				180 00

2.

CASH RECEIPTS JOURNAL

PAGE 8

DATE		ACCOUNT TITLE	DOC. NO.	POST. REF.	1 GENERAL DEBIT	2 GENERAL CREDIT	3 ACCOUNTS RECEIVABLE CREDIT	4 SALES CREDIT	5 SALES TAX PAYABLE CREDIT	6 SALES DISCOUNT DEBIT	7 CASH DEBIT
20X4 Jan.	2	*Accum. Depr.—Store Equip.*	*R11*		1950 00						4000 00
		Store Equipment				5600 00					
		Gain on Plant Assets				350 00					
Oct.	3	*Accum. Depr.—Office Equip.*	*R255*		800 00						325 00
		Loss on Plant Assets			125 00						
		Office Equipment				1250 00					

Name ____________ Date ________ Class ________

18-5 WORK TOGETHER, p. 554

Calculating depreciation using the double declining-balance depreciation method

Plant asset: *Truck* | Original cost: *$22,000.00*
Depreciation method: *Double declining-balance* | Estimated salvage value: *$ 2,200.00*
Estimated useful life: *4 years*

Year	Beginning Book Value	Declining-Balance Rate	Annual Depreciation	Ending Book Value
1	$22,000.00	50%	$11,000.00	$11,000.00
2	11,000.00	50%	5,500.00	5,500.00
3	5,500.00	50%	2,750.00	2,750.00
4	2,750.00	50%	550.00	2,200.00

Plant asset: *Cash Register* | Original cost: *$1,200.00*
Depreciation method: *Double declining-balance* | Estimated salvage value: *$ 100.00*
Estimated useful life: *5 years*

Year	Beginning Book Value	Declining-Balance Rate	Annual Depreciation	Ending Book Value
1	$1,200.00	40%	$480.00	$720.00
2	720.00	40%	288.00	432.00
3	432.00	40%	172.80	259.20
4	259.20	40%	103.68	155.52
5	155.52	40%	55.52	100.00

Plant asset: *Clothing Rack* | Original cost: *$500.00*
Depreciation method: *Double declining-balance* | Estimated salvage value: *$ 50.00*
Estimated useful life: *8 years*

Year	Beginning Book Value	Declining-Balance Rate	Annual Depreciation	Ending Book Value
1	$500.00	25%	$125.00	$375.00
2	375.00	25%	93.75	281.25
3	281.25	25%	70.31	210.94
4	210.94	25%	52.74	158.20
5	158.20	25%	39.55	118.65
6	118.65	25%	29.66	88.99
7	88.99	25%	22.25	66.74
8	66.74	25%	16.74	50.00

18-5 ON YOUR OWN, p. 554

Calculating depreciation using the double declining-balance depreciation method

Plant asset: *Ski Rack*
Depreciation method: *Double declining-balance*
Original cost: *$1,200.00*
Estimated salvage value: *$ 100.00*
Estimated useful life: *5 years*

Year	Beginning Book Value	Declining-Balance Rate	Annual Depreciation	Ending Book Value
1	$1,200.00	40%	$480.00	$720.00
2	720.00	40%	288.00	432.00
3	432.00	40%	172.80	259.20
4	259.20	40%	103.68	155.52
5	155.52	40%	55.52	100.00

Plant asset: *Delivery Truck*
Depreciation method: *Double declining-balance*
Original cost: *$25,000.00*
Estimated salvage value: *$ 2,000.00*
Estimated useful life: *3 years*

Year	Beginning Book Value	Declining-Balance Rate	Annual Depreciation	Ending Book Value
1	$25,000.00	66.67%	$16,667.50	$8,332.50
2	8,332.50	66.67%	5,555.28	2,777.22
3	2,777.22	66.67%	777.22	2,000.00

Plant asset: *Filing Cabinet*
Depreciation method: *Double declining-balance*
Original cost: *$600.00*
Estimated salvage value: *$ 50.00*
Estimated useful life: *4 years*

Year	Beginning Book Value	Declining-Balance Rate	Annual Depreciation	Ending Book Value
1	$600.00	50%	$300.00	$300.00
2	300.00	50%	150.00	150.00
3	150.00	50%	75.00	75.00
4	75.00	50%	25.00	50.00

Name ______ Date ______ Class ______

18-1 APPLICATION PROBLEM, p. 556

Journalizing buying plant assets and paying property tax

1., 2.

CASH PAYMENTS JOURNAL

PAGE 1

	DATE		ACCOUNT TITLE	CK. NO.	POST. REF.	1 GENERAL DEBIT	2 GENERAL CREDIT	3 ACCOUNTS PAYABLE DEBIT	4 PURCHASES DISCOUNT CREDIT	5 CASH CREDIT	
1	20-- Jan.	4	Office Equipment	334	1205	700 00				700 00	1
2		5	Store Equipment	337	1215	4 200 00				4 200 00	2
3	Feb.	24	Property Tax Expense	411	6145	3 360 00				3 360 00	3
4	May	12	Store Equipment	534	1215	1 250 00				1 250 00	4
5											5

2.

GENERAL LEDGER

ACCOUNT Office Equipment ACCOUNT NO. 1205

DATE		ITEM	POST. REF.	DEBIT	CREDIT	BALANCE DEBIT	BALANCE CREDIT
20-- Jan.	1	Balance	✔			15 848 50	
	4		CP1	700 00		16 548 50	

ACCOUNT Store Equipment ACCOUNT NO. 1215

DATE		ITEM	POST. REF.	DEBIT	CREDIT	BALANCE DEBIT	BALANCE CREDIT
20-- Jan.	1	Balance	✔			82 483 75	
	5		CP1	4 200 00		86 683 75	
May	12		CP1	1 250 00		87 933 75	

ACCOUNT Property Tax Expense ACCOUNT NO. 6145

DATE		ITEM	POST. REF.	DEBIT	CREDIT	BALANCE DEBIT	BALANCE CREDIT
20-- Feb.	24		CP1	3 360 00		3 360 00	

18-2 APPLICATION PROBLEM, p. 556

Calculating straight-line depreciation

Plant asset:	*Cooler*	Original cost:	*$1,400.00*
Depreciation method:	*Straight-line*	Estimated salvage value:	*$ 350.00*
		Estimated useful life:	*7 years*

Year	Beginning Book Value	Annual Depreciation	Accumulated Depreciation	Ending Book Value
20X1	$1,400.00	$150.00	$ 150.00	$1,250.00
20X2	1,250.00	150.00	300.00	1,100.00
20X3	1,100.00	150.00	450.00	950.00
20X4	950.00	150.00	600.00	800.00
20X5	800.00	150.00	750.00	650.00
20X6	650.00	150.00	900.00	500.00
20X7	500.00	150.00	1,050.00	350.00

Plant asset:	*Office Chair*	Original cost:	*$500.00*
Depreciation method:	*Straight-line*	Estimated salvage value:	*$ 50.00*
		Estimated useful life:	*5 years*

Year	Beginning Book Value	Annual Depreciation	Accumulated Depreciation	Ending Book Value
20X1	$500.00	$67.50	$ 67.50	$432.50
20X2	432.50	90.00	157.50	342.50
20X3	342.50	90.00	247.50	252.50
20X4	252.50	90.00	337.50	162.50
20X5	162.50	90.00	427.50	72.50
20X6	72.50	22.50	450.00	50.00

Plant asset:	*Sale Sign*	Original cost:	*$350.00*
Depreciation method:	*Straight-line*	Estimated salvage value:	*$ 50.00*
		Estimated useful life:	*5 years*

Year	Beginning Book Value	Annual Depreciation	Accumulated Depreciation	Ending Book Value
20X1	$350.00	$25.00	$ 25.00	$325.00
20X2	325.00	60.00	85.00	265.00
20X3	265.00	60.00	145.00	205.00
20X4	205.00	60.00	205.00	145.00
20X5	145.00	60.00	265.00	85.00
20X6	85.00	35.00	300.00	50.00

Name ______________________ Date ____________ Class ____________

18-3 APPLICATION PROBLEM, p. 556

Preparing plant asset records

These plant asset records are needed to complete Application Problem 18-5.

PLANT ASSET RECORD No. 311 General Ledger Account No. 1215

Description *Cooler* General Ledger Account Store Equipment

Date Bought *January 4, 20X1* Serial Number *47367BX34* Original Cost *$1,400.00*

Estimated Useful Life *7 years* Estimated Salvage Value *$350.00* Depreciation Method *Straight-line*

18-3

Disposed of: Discarded ______ Sold *✔* Traded ______

Date *July 8, 20X5* Disposal Amount *$300.00*

18-5

Year	Annual Depreciation Expense	Accumulated Depreciation	Ending Book Value
20X1	*$150.00*	*$150.00*	*$1,250.00*
20X2	*150.00*	*300.00*	*1,100.00*
20X3	*150.00*	*450.00*	*950.00*
20X4	*150.00*	*600.00*	*800.00*
20X5	*75.00*	*675.00*	*725.00*

Continue record on back of card

18-3 (20X1–20X4) · 18-5 (20X5)

PLANT ASSET RECORD No. 312 | General Ledger Account No. 1205

Description *Office Chair* | General Ledger Account Office Equipment

Date Bought *March 30, 20X1* | Serial Number *1727X6B3* | Original Cost *$500.00*

Estimated Useful Life *5 years* | Estimated Salvage Value *$50.00* | Depreciation Method *Straight-line*

18-3

Disposed of: Discarded ____ Sold ✔ Traded ____

Date *January 6, 20X5* | Disposal Amount *$250.00*

18-5

Year	Annual Depreciation Expense	Accumulated Depreciation	Ending Book Value
20X1	$67.50	$ 67.50	$432.50
20X2	90.00	157.50	342.50
20X3	90.00	247.50	252.50
20X4	90.00	337.50	162.50

18-3

Continue record on back of card

18-3 APPLICATION PROBLEM (concluded)

PLANT ASSET RECORD No. 313 — General Ledger Account No. 1215

Description *Sale Sign* — General Ledger Account Store Equipment

Date Bought *August 2, 20X1* — Serial Number *BC762761* — Original Cost *$350.00*

Estimated Useful Life *5 years* — Estimated Salvage Value *$50.00* — Depreciation Method *Straight-line*

18-3

Disposed of: Discarded ______ Sold ✔ Traded ______

Date *March 29, 20X5* — Disposal Amount *$130.00*

18-5

Year	Annual Depreciation Expense	Accumulated Depreciation	Ending Book Value
20X1	*$25.00*	*$ 25.00*	*$325.00*
20X2	*60.00*	*85.00*	*265.00*
20X3	*60.00*	*145.00*	*205.00*
20X4	*60.00*	*205.00*	*145.00*
20X5	*15.00*	*220.00*	*130.00*

(Rows 20X1–20X4: 18-3; Row 20X5: 18-5)

Continue record on back of card

18-4 APPLICATION PROBLEM, p. 557

Journalizing annual depreciation expense

Ester Engineering, Inc.

Work Sheet

For Year Ended December 31, 20 – –

	ACCOUNT TITLE	1 TRIAL BALANCE DEBIT	2 TRIAL BALANCE CREDIT	3 ADJUSTMENTS DEBIT	4 ADJUSTMENTS CREDIT
10	Office Equipment	51 2 4 8 25			
11	Accumulated Depreciation—Office Equipment		31 0 0 5 00		(f) 4 3 2 0 00
38	Depreciation Expense—Office Equipment			(f) 4 3 2 0 00	

GENERAL LEDGER

ACCOUNT Office Equipment ACCOUNT NO. 1205

DATE		ITEM	POST. REF.	DEBIT	CREDIT	BALANCE DEBIT	BALANCE CREDIT
20-- Dec.	31	Balance	✔			51 2 4 8 25	

ACCOUNT Accumulated Depreciation—Office Equipment ACCOUNT NO. 1210

DATE		ITEM	POST. REF.	DEBIT	CREDIT	BALANCE DEBIT	BALANCE CREDIT
20-- Dec.	31	Balance	✔				31 0 0 5 00
	31		G14		4 3 2 0 00		35 3 2 5 00

ACCOUNT Depreciation Expense—Office Equipment ACCOUNT NO. 6120

DATE		ITEM	POST. REF.	DEBIT	CREDIT	BALANCE DEBIT	BALANCE CREDIT
20-- Dec.	31		G14	4 3 2 0 00		4 3 2 0 00	

Name ______________________ Date ______________ Class ______________

18-4 APPLICATION PROBLEM (concluded)

GENERAL JOURNAL PAGE 14

	DATE		ACCOUNT TITLE	DOC. NO.	POST. REF.	DEBIT	CREDIT	
1			*Adjusting Entries*					1
2	*20-- Dec.*	*31*	*Depreciation Expense—Office Equipment*		*6120*	*4 3 2 0 00*		2
3			*Accumulated Depreciation—Office Equipment*		*1210*		*4 3 2 0 00*	3
4								4
5								5

Recording the disposal of plant assets

1.

GENERAL JOURNAL — PAGE 3

	DATE		ACCOUNT TITLE	DOC. NO.	POST. REF.	DEBIT	CREDIT	
1	20X5 Mar.	29	Depreciation Expense—Store Equipment	M3		15 00		1
2			Accumulated Depreciation—Store Equipment				15 00	2
3	July	8	Depreciation Expense—Store Equipment	M34		75 00		3
4			Accumulated Depreciation—Store Equipment				75 00	4
5								5

2.

CASH RECEIPTS JOURNAL — PAGE 3

	DATE		ACCOUNT TITLE	DOC. NO.	POST. REF.	1 GENERAL DEBIT	2 GENERAL CREDIT	3 ACCOUNTS RECEIVABLE CREDIT	4 SALES CREDIT	5 SALES TAX PAYABLE CREDIT	6 SALES DISCOUNT DEBIT	7 CASH DEBIT	
1	20X5 Jan.	6	Accum. Depr.—Office Equip.	R4		337 50						250 00	1
2			Office Equipment				500 00						2
3			Gain on Plant Assets				87 50						3
4	Mar.	29	Accum. Depr.—Store Equip.	R53		220 00						130 00	4
5			Store Equipment				350 00						5
6	July	8	Accum. Depr.—Store Equip.	R125		675 00						300 00	6
7			Loss on Plant Assets			425 00							7
8			Store Equipment				1400 00						8
9													9
10													10
11													11
12													12
13													13

Name ____________ Date ____________ Class ____________

18-6 APPLICATION PROBLEM, p. 557

Calculating depreciation using the double declining-balance depreciation method

Plant asset:	*Display Case*	Original cost:	*$1,600.00*
Depreciation method:	*Double declining-balance*	Estimated salvage value:	*$ 200.00*
		Estimated useful life:	*8 years*

Year	Beginning Book Value	Declining-Balance Rate	Annual Depreciation	Ending Book Value
1	*$1,600.00*	*25%*	*$400.00*	*$1,200.00*
2	*1,200.00*	*25%*	*300.00*	*900.00*
3	*900.00*	*25%*	*225.00*	*675.00*
4	*675.00*	*25%*	*168.75*	*506.25*
5	*506.25*	*25%*	*126.56*	*379.69*
6	*379.69*	*25%*	*94.92*	*284.77*
7	*284.77*	*25%*	*71.19*	*213.58*
8	*213.58*	*25%*	*13.58*	*200.00*

Plant asset:	*Truck*	Original cost:	*$30,000.00*
Depreciation method:	*Double declining-balance*	Estimated salvage value:	*$ 2,500.00*
		Estimated useful life:	*4 years*

Year	Beginning Book Value	Declining-Balance Rate	Annual Depreciation	Ending Book Value
1	*$30,000.00*	*50%*	*$15,000.00*	*$15,000.00*
2	*15,000.00*	*50%*	*7,500.00*	*7,500.00*
3	*7,500.00*	*50%*	*3,750.00*	*3,750.00*
4	*3,750.00*	*50%*	*1,250.00*	*2,500.00*

Plant asset:	*Mixer*	Original cost:	*$2,400.00*
Depreciation method:	*Double declining-balance*	Estimated salvage value:	*$ 300.00*
		Estimated useful life:	*5 years*

Year	Beginning Book Value	Declining-Balance Rate	Annual Depreciation	Ending Book Value
1	*$2,400.00*	*40%*	*$960.00*	*$1,440.00*
2	*1,440.00*	*40%*	*576.00*	*864.00*
3	*864.00*	*40%*	*345.60*	*518.40*
4	*518.40*	*40%*	*207.36*	*311.04*
5	*311.04*	*40%*	*11.04*	*300.00*

18-7 MASTERY PROBLEM, pp. 557, 558

Recording transactions for plant assets

1.

CASH PAYMENTS JOURNAL — PAGE 1

	DATE		ACCOUNT TITLE	CK. NO.	POST. REF.	1 GENERAL DEBIT	2 GENERAL CREDIT	3 ACCOUNTS PAYABLE DEBIT	4 PURCHASES DISCOUNT CREDIT	5 CASH CREDIT	
1	20X1 Jan.	5	Room Furnishings	435		2 200 00				2 200 00	1
2	Feb.	26	Property Tax Expense	534		12 800 00				12 800 00	2
3	Apr.	5	Equipment	577		1 300 00				1 300 00	3
4											4
5											5
6											6

Name ______________________ Date ____________ Class ____________

18-7 MASTERY PROBLEM (continued)

2., 4., 6.

PLANT ASSET RECORD No. *892* General Ledger Account No. *1205*

Description *Dining Table* General Ledger Account *Room Furnishings*

Date Bought *January 5, 20X1* Serial Number *903452* Original Cost *$2,200.00*

Estimated Useful Life *5 years* Estimated Salvage Value *$200.00* Depreciation Method *Double declining-balance*

Disposed of: Discarded ______ Sold ✔ Traded ______

Date *January 6, 20X5* Disposal Amount *$300.00*

Year	Annual Depreciation Expense	Accumulated Depreciation	Ending Book Value
20X1	$880.00	$ 880.00	$1,320.00
20X2	528.00	1,408.00	792.00
20X3	316.80	1,724.80	475.20
20X4	190.08	1,914.88	285.12

PLANT ASSET RECORD No. *893* General Ledger Account No. *1215*

Description *Air Purifier* General Ledger Account *Equipment*

Date Bought *April 5, 20X1* Serial Number *BE35CC* Original Cost *$1,300.00*

Estimated Useful Life *6 years* Estimated Salvage Value *$100.00* Depreciation Method *Straight-line*

Disposed of: Discarded ______ Sold ✔ Traded ______

Date *July 2, 20X5* Disposal Amount *$200.00*

Year	Annual Depreciation Expense	Accumulated Depreciation	Ending Book Value
20X1	$150.00	$150.00	$1,150.00
20X2	200.00	350.00	950.00
20X3	200.00	550.00	750.00
20X4	200.00	750.00	550.00
20X5	100.00	850.00	450.00

18-7 MASTERY PROBLEM (continued)

3.

Plant asset:	*Dining Table*	Original cost:	*$2,200.00*
Depreciation method:	*Double declining-balance*	Estimated salvage value:	*$ 200.00*
		Estimated useful life:	*5 years*

Year	Beginning Book Value	Declining-Balance Rate	Annual Depreciation	Ending Book Value
20X1	*$2,200.00*	*40%*	*$880.00*	*$1,320.00*
20X2	*1,320.00*	*40%*	*528.00*	*792.00*
20X3	*792.00*	*40%*	*316.80*	*475.20*
20X4	*475.20*	*40%*	*190.08*	*285.12*
20X5	*285.12*	*40%*	*85.12*	*200.00*

Plant asset:	*Air Purifier*	Original cost:	*$1,300.00*
Depreciation method:	*Straight-line*	Estimated salvage value:	*$ 100.00*
		Estimated useful life:	*6 years*

Year	Beginning Book Value	Annual Depreciation	Accumulated Depreciation	Ending Book Value
1	*$1,300.00*	*$150.00*	*$ 150.00*	*$1,150.00*
2	*1,150.00*	*200.00*	*350.00*	*950.00*
3	*950.00*	*200.00*	*550.00*	*750.00*
4	*750.00*	*200.00*	*750.00*	*550.00*
5	*550.00*	*200.00*	*950.00*	*350.00*
6	*350.00*	*200.00*	*1,150.00*	*150.00*
7	*150.00*	*50.00*	*1,200.00*	*100.00*

Name ______________________ Date ______________ Class ______________

18-7 MASTERY PROBLEM (concluded)

5.

CASH RECEIPTS JOURNAL

PAGE 2

	DATE		ACCOUNT TITLE	DOC. NO.	POST. REF.	1 GENERAL DEBIT	2 GENERAL CREDIT	3 ACCOUNTS RECEIVABLE CREDIT	4 SALES CREDIT	5 SALES TAX PAYABLE CREDIT	6 SALES DISCOUNT DEBIT	7 CASH DEBIT	
1	20X5 Jan.	6	Accum. Depr.—Room Furnishing	R4		1914 88						300 00	1
2			Room Furnishings				2200 00						2
3			Gain on Plant Assets				14 88						3
4	July	2	Accum. Depr.—Equipment	R77		850 00						200 00	4
5			Loss on Plant Assets			250 00							5
6			Equipment				1300 00						6

GENERAL JOURNAL

PAGE 18

	DATE		ACCOUNT TITLE	DOC. NO.	POST. REF.	DEBIT	CREDIT	
1	20X5 July	2	Depreciation Expense—Equipment	M31		100 00		1
2			Accumulated Depreciation—Equipment				100 00	2
3			Adjusting Entries					3
4	Dec.	31	Depreciation Expense—Room Furnishings			3852 00		4
5			Accumulated Depreciation—Room Furnishings				3852 00	5

18-8 CHALLENGE PROBLEM, p. 558

Calculating a partial year's depreciation using the double declining-balance method

Plant asset:	*Lift*	Original cost:	*$3,600.00*
Depreciation method:	*Double declining-balance*	Estimated salvage value:	*$ 250.00*
		Estimated useful life:	*5 years*

Year	Beginning Book Value	Declining-Balance Rate	Annual Depreciation	Ending Book Value
1	*$3,600.00*	*40%*	*$1,080.00*	*$2,520.00*
2	*2,520.00*	*40%*	*1,008.00*	*1,512.00*
3	*1,512.00*	*40%*	*604.80*	*907.20*
4	*907.20*	*40%*	*362.88*	*544.32*
5	*544.32*	*40%*	*217.73*	*326.59*
6	*326.59*	*40%*	*76.59*	*250.00*

Plant asset:	*Lawnmower*	Original cost:	*$5,400.00*
Depreciation method:	*Double declining-balance*	Estimated salvage value:	*$ 300.00*
		Estimated useful life:	*4 years*

Year	Beginning Book Value	Declining-Balance Rate	Annual Depreciation	Ending Book Value
1	*$5,400.00*	*50%*	*$1,125.00*	*$4,275.00*
2	*4,275.00*	*50%*	*2,137.50*	*2,137.50*
3	*2,137.50*	*50%*	*1,068.75*	*1,068.75*
4	*1,068.75*	*50%*	*534.38*	*534.37*
5	*534.37*	*50%*	*234.37*	*300.00*

Study Guide 19

Name	Perfect Score	Your Score
Identifying Accounting Terms	9 Pts.	
Analyzing Inventory Systems	10 Pts.	
Analyzing Lifo, Fifo, and Weighted-Average Methods	12 Pts.	
Total	31 Pts.	

Part One—Identifying Accounting Terms

Directions: Select the one term in Column I that best fits each definition in Column II. Print the letter identifying your choice in the Answers column.

Column I

A. first-in, first-out inventory costing method
B. gross profit method of estimating inventory
C. inventory record
D. last-in, first-out inventory costing method
E. periodic inventory
F. perpetual inventory
G. stock ledger
H. stock record
I. weighted-average inventory costing method

Column II	Answers
1. A merchandise inventory determined by counting, weighing, or measuring items of merchandise on hand. (p. 565)	1. *E*
2. A merchandise inventory determined by keeping a continuous record of increases, decreases, and balance on hand. (p. 565)	2. *F*
3. A form used during a periodic inventory to record information about each item of merchandise on hand. (p. 566)	3. *C*
4. A form used to show the kind of merchandise, quantity received, quantity sold, and balance on hand. (p. 567)	4. *H*
5. A file of stock records for all merchandise on hand. (p. 567)	5. *G*
6. Using the price of merchandise purchased first to calculate the cost of merchandise sold first. (p. 569)	6. *A*
7. Using the price of merchandise purchased last to calculate the cost of merchandise sold first. (p. 570)	7. *D*
8. Using the average cost of beginning inventory plus merchandise purchased during a fiscal period to calculate the cost of merchandise sold. (p. 571)	8. *I*
9. Estimating inventory by using the previous year's percentage of gross profit on operations. (p. 574)	9. *B*

Part Two—Analyzing Inventory Systems

Directions: Place a *T* for True or an *F* for False in the Answers column to show whether each of the following statements is true or false.

	Answers
1. Merchandise inventory on hand is typically the largest current asset of a merchandising business. (p. 564)	1. *T*
2. The only financial statement on which the value of merchandise on hand is reported is the income statement. (p. 564)	2. *F*
3. Net income of a business can be decreased by maintaining a merchandise inventory that is larger than needed. (p. 565)	3. *T*
4. A perpetual inventory is sometimes known as a physical inventory. (p. 565)	4. *F*
5. A minimum inventory balance is the amount of merchandise that will typically last until ordered merchandise can be received from vendors. (p. 565)	5. *T*
6. A perpetual inventory system provides day-to-day information about the quality of merchandise on hand. (p. 567)	6. *F*
7. A periodic inventory should be taken at least once a month, even when perpetual inventory records are kept. (p. 567)	7. *F*
8. Some cash registers use optical scanners to read the UPC codes marked on products. (p. 567)	8. *T*
9. First-in, first-out is a method used to determine the quantity of each type of merchandise on hand. (p. 569)	9. *F*
10. The gross profit method makes it possible to prepare monthly income statements without taking a periodic inventory. (p. 574)	10. *T*

Name ________________________ Date ____________ Class ____________

Part Three—Analyzing Lifo, Fifo, and Weighted-Average Methods

Directions: For each of the following items, select the choice that best completes the statement. Print the letter identifying your choice in the Answers column.

		Answers
1.	Calculating an accurate inventory cost to assure that gross profit and net income are reported correctly on the income statement is an application of the accounting concept (A) Consistent Reporting (B) Perpetual Inventory (C) Adequate Disclosure (D) none of these (p. 564)	**1.** *C*
2.	When the fifo method is used, cost of merchandise sold is valued at the (A) average price (B) most recent price (C) earliest price (D) none of these (p. 569)	**2.** *C*
3.	The fifo method is based on the assumption that the merchandise purchased first is the merchandise (A) sold first (B) sold last (C) in beginning inventory (D) none of these (p. 569)	**3.** *A*
4.	When the fifo method is used, ending inventory units are priced at the (A) average price (B) earliest price (C) most recent price (D) none of these (p. 569)	**4.** *C*
5.	Using an inventory costing method that charges the most recent costs of merchandise against current revenue is an application of the accounting concept (A) Adequate Disclosure (B) Consistent Reporting (C) Matching Expenses with Revenue (D) none of these (p. 570)	**5.** *C*
6.	The lifo method is based on the assumption that the merchandise purchased last is the merchandise (A) sold first (B) sold last (C) in ending inventory (D) none of these (p. 570)	**6.** *A*
7.	When the lifo method is used, cost of merchandise sold is priced at the (A) average price (B) earliest price (C) most recent price (D) none of these (p. 570)	**7.** *C*
8.	The weighted-average method is based on the assumption that the cost of merchandise sold should be calculated using the (A) average price per unit of beginning inventory (B) average price of ending inventory (C) average price of beginning inventory plus purchases during the fiscal period (D) average price of ending inventory plus purchases during the fiscal period (p. 571)	**8.** *C*
9.	When the weighted-average method is used, ending inventory units are priced at the (A) earliest price (B) most recent price (C) average price (D) none of these (p. 571)	**9.** *C*
10.	A business that uses the same inventory costing method for all fiscal periods is applying the accounting concept (A) Consistent Reporting (B) Accounting Period Cycle (C) Perpetual Inventory (D) Adequate Disclosure (p. 572)	**10.** *A*
11.	In a year of rising prices, the inventory method that gives the lowest possible value for ending inventory is (A) fifo (B) lifo (C) weighted-average (D) gross profit (p. 572)	**11.** *B*
12.	In a year of falling prices, the inventory method that gives the lowest possible value for ending inventory is (A) weighted-average (B) lifo (C) fifo (D) gross profit (p. 572)	**12.** *C*

Study Skills

Using the Library

Being able to use the library properly is an invaluable skill for anyone. You should visit the library in your school or community often and take as much time as necessary to become thoroughly familiar with every section.

Never be afraid to ask for help. Any librarian should be happy to help you locate any information that you need. If you don't know where to look for information, ask someone to help you. If you can't find information, ask for assistance. If you don't know how to use special equipment, ask for a demonstration.

The Catalog System

Most libraries use either the Library of Congress System or the Dewey Decimal System. Determine which system your library uses and obtain a floor plan of the library to determine where each section is housed. A floor plan is usually available at the main circulation desk, at each entrance to the building, and near the stairs. Take some time to become familiar with every area; it will save you time later when you want to locate a book.

Texts

If you are preparing to write a paper in a particular subject area, you should become familiar with the texts in that field. You may be able to find a number of books on your topic located in one section of the library.

Reference Books

Your library probably has many types of reference books. In the reference section of your library, you will find such books as atlases, encyclopedias, dictionaries, and various other sources of information. In reference books, you will be able to find information on people, places, and events that you may need for your paper.

Periodicals

You will often want to obtain current information on a subject—information that is less than a year old. Current information may be found in the latest issues of periodicals. Your library probably has a collection of newspapers, magazines, and professional journals that you can use when you need current references.

In addition to the latest issues, you may want to read old newspaper and journal articles. Sometimes the library has actual copies of old papers and journals, and sometimes information is available on microfilm.

Electronic Sources

Your library also subscribes to databases which contain vast amounts of information that is available through a computer terminal. The database may be located in another city or another area of the country; however, you will be able to locate information quickly and easily using a computer. You can even obtain a printed copy by using a printer at your computer terminal.

Make the Most of Your Library

The information in the library is usually available to anyone who wants to use it. The library is a vast source of information and enjoyment. Use it often and well.

Name ______________________ Date ____________ Class ____________

19-1 WORK TOGETHER, p. 568

Preparing a stock record

1.

STOCK RECORD

Description 16-Gauge Speaker Wire Stock No. W-394
Reorder 750 Minimum 300 Location Bin T37

1	2	3	4	5	6	7
INCREASES			DECREASES			BALANCE
DATE	PURCHASE INVOICE NO.	QUANTITY	DATE	SALES INVOICE NO.	QUANTITY	QUANTITY
			Sept. 15	2490	150	400
			Oct. 3	*2543*	*250*	*150*
Oct. 27	*1542*	*750*				*900*
			Oct. 29	*2654*	*300*	*600*
			Dec. 4	*2801*	*170*	*430*

19-1 ON YOUR OWN, p. 568

Preparing a stock record

1.

STOCK RECORD

Description 8″ x 10″ white metal frame Stock No. M-253
Reorder 50 Minimum 20 Location Bin F45

1	2	3	4	5	6	7
INCREASES			DECREASES			BALANCE
DATE	PURCHASE INVOICE NO.	QUANTITY	DATE	SALES INVOICE NO.	QUANTITY	QUANTITY
			Oct. 30	543	20	45
			Nov. 4	*590*	*10*	*35*
			Nov. 16	*624*	*25*	*10*
Nov. 22	*223*	*50*				*60*
			Dec. 9	*645*	*15*	*45*

19-2 WORK TOGETHER, p. 573

Determining the cost of inventory using the fifo, lifo, and weighted-average inventory costing methods

1.

FIFO Method

Purchase Dates	Units Purchased	Unit Price	Total Cost	FIFO Units on Hand	FIFO Cost
January 1, beginning inventory	14	$30.00	$ 420.00		
March 29, purchases	9	32.00	288.00		
May 6, purchases	10	34.00	340.00		
August 28, purchases	8	36.00	288.00	*7*	*$252.00*
November 8, purchases	9	38.00	342.00	*9*	*342.00*
Totals	50		$1,678.00	*16*	*$594.00*

LIFO Method

Purchase Dates	Units Purchased	Unit Price	Total Cost	LIFO Units on Hand	LIFO Cost
January 1, beginning inventory	14	$30.00	$ 420.00	*14*	*$420.00*
March 29, purchases	9	32.00	288.00	*2*	*64.00*
May 6, purchases	10	34.00	340.00		
August 28, purchases	8	36.00	288.00		
November 8, purchases	9	38.00	342.00		
Totals	50		$1,678.00	*16*	*$484.00*

Weighted-Average Method

Purchases			Total Cost
Date	Units	Unit Price	
January 1, beginning inventory	14	$30.00	*$ 420.00*
March 29, purchases	9	32.00	*288.00*
May 6, purchases	10	34.00	*340.00*
August 28, purchases	8	36.00	*288.00*
November 8, purchases	9	38.00	*342.00*
Totals	50		*$1,678.00*

Total of Beginning Inventory and Purchases	÷	*Total Units*	=	*Weighted-Average Price per Unit*
$1,678.00		*50*		*$33.56*

Units in Ending Inventory	×	*Weighted-Average Price per Unit*	=	*Cost of Ending Inventory*
16		*$33.56*		*$536.96*

Name ______________________ Date ____________ Class ____________

19-2 ON YOUR OWN, p. 573

Determining the cost of inventory using the fifo, lifo, and weighted-average inventory costing methods

1.

FIFO Method

Purchase Dates	Units Purchased	Unit Price	Total Cost	FIFO Units on Hand	FIFO Cost
January 1, beginning inventory	18	$4.60	$ 82.80		
April 9, purchases	12	4.70	56.40		
June 12, purchases	14	4.80	67.20		
September 22, purchases	15	5.00	75.00	*8*	*$ 40.00*
November 20, purchases	16	5.10	81.60	*16*	*81.60*
Totals	75		$363.00	*24*	*$121.60*

LIFO Method

Purchase Dates	Units Purchased	Unit Price	Total Cost	LIFO Units on Hand	LIFO Cost
January 1, beginning inventory	18	$4.60	$ 82.80	*18*	*$ 82.80*
April 9, purchases	12	4.70	56.40	*6*	*28.20*
June 12, purchases	14	4.80	67.20		
September 22, purchases	15	5.00	75.00		
November 20, purchases	16	5.10	81.60		
Totals	75		$363.00	*24*	*$111.00*

Weighted-Average Method

Purchases			Total Cost
Date	Units	Unit Price	
January 1, beginning inventory	18	$4.60	*$ 82.80*
April 9, purchases	12	4.70	*56.40*
June 12, purchases	14	4.80	*67.20*
September 22, purchases	15	5.00	*75.00*
November 20, purchases	16	5.10	*81.60*
Totals	75		*$363.00*

Total of Beginning Inventory and Purchases	÷	*Total Units*	=	*Weighted-Average Price per Unit*
$363.00		*75*		*$4.84*

Units in Ending Inventory	×	*Weighted-Average Price per Unit*	=	*Cost of Ending Inventory*
24		*$4.84*		*$116.16*

19-3 WORK TOGETHER, p. 576

Estimating ending inventory using the gross profit method

1.

STEP 1	
Beginning inventory, June 1	$154,800.00
Plus net purchases for June 1 to June 30	+ 47,800.00
Equals cost of merchandise available for sale	$202,600.00
STEP 2	
Net sales for June 1 to June 30	$245,000.00
Times previous year's gross profit percentage	× 45.0%
Equals estimated gross profit on operations	$110,250.00
STEP 3	
Net sales for June 1 to June 30	$245,000.00
Less estimated gross profit on operations	−110,250.00
Equals estimated cost of merchandise sold	$134,750.00
STEP 4	
Cost of merchandise available for sale	$202,600.00
Less estimated cost of merchandise sold	−134,750.00
Equals estimated ending merchandise inventory	$ 67,850.00

2.

Evans Company

Income Statement

For Month Ended June 30, 20 – –

			% OF NET SALES
Operating Revenue:			
Net Sales		245 000 00	100.0
Cost of Merchandise Sold:			
Estimated Beginning Inventory, June 1	154 800 00		
Net Purchases	47 800 00		
Merchandise Available for Sale	202 600 00		
Less Estimated Ending Inventory, June 30	67 850 00		
Cost of Merchandise Sold		134 750 00	55.0
Gross Profit on Operations		110 250 00	45.0
Operating Expenses		76 930 00	31.4
Net Income		33 320 00	13.6

Name ______________________ Date ____________ Class ____________

19-3 ON YOUR OWN, p. 576

Estimating ending inventory using the gross profit method

1.

STEP 1	
Beginning inventory, April 1	$24,500.00
Plus net purchases for April 1 to April 30	+12,100.00
Equals cost of merchandise available for sale	$36,600.00
STEP 2	
Net sales for April 1 to April 30	$56,000.00
Times previous year's gross profit percentage	× 55.0%
Equals estimated gross profit on operations	$30,800.00
STEP 3	
Net sales for April 1 to April 30	$56,000.00
Less estimated gross profit on operations	−30,800.00
Equals estimated cost of merchandise sold	$25,200.00
STEP 4	
Cost of merchandise available for sale	$36,600.00
Less estimated cost of merchandise sold	−25,200.00
Equals estimated ending merchandise inventory	$11,400.00

2.

Luke Enterprises

Income Statement

For Month Ended April 30, 20 – –

			% OF NET SALES
Operating Revenue:			
Net Sales		56,000.00	100.0
Cost of Merchandise Sold:			
Estimated Beginning Inventory, April 1	24,500.00		
Net Purchases	12,100.00		
Merchandise Available for Sale	36,600.00		
Less Estimated Ending Inventory, April 30	11,400.00		
Cost of Merchandise Sold		25,200.00	45.0
Gross Profit on Operations		30,800.00	55.0
Operating Expenses		17,920.00	32.0
Net Income		12,880.00	23.0

19-1 APPLICATION PROBLEM, p. 578

Preparing a stock record

STOCK RECORD

Description 450-gallon spa Stock No. HT-450

Reorder 5 Minimum 2 Location Area A-4

1	2	3	4	5	6	7
INCREASES			DECREASES			BALANCE
DATE	PURCHASE INVOICE NO.	QUANTITY	DATE	SALES INVOICE NO.	QUANTITY	QUANTITY
			Jan. 3	2399	1	4
			Feb. 4	*2433*	*1*	*3*
			Feb. 28	*2478*	*2*	*1*
Mar. 10	*789*	*5*				*6*
			Mar. 24	*2502*	*1*	*5*

Name ____________________ Date ____________ Class ____________

19-2 APPLICATION PROBLEM, p. 578

Determining the cost of inventory using the fifo, lifo, and weighted-average inventory costing methods

FIFO Method

Purchase Dates	Units Purchased	Unit Price	Total Cost	FIFO Units on Hand	FIFO Cost
January 1, beginning inventory	90	$2.00	$180.00		
March 13, purchases	78	2.10	163.80		
June 8, purchases	80	2.25	180.00		
September 16, purchases	84	2.30	193.20	*84*	*$193.20*
December 22, purchases	88	2.40	211.20	*88*	*211.20*
Totals	420		$928.20	*172*	*$404.40*

LIFO Method

Purchase Dates	Units Purchased	Unit Price	Total Cost	LIFO Units on Hand	LIFO Cost
January 1, beginning inventory	90	$2.00	$180.00	*90*	*$180.00*
March 13, purchases	78	2.10	163.80	*78*	*163.80*
June 8, purchases	80	2.25	180.00	*4*	*9.00*
September 16, purchases	84	2.30	193.20		
December 22, purchases	88	2.40	211.20		
Totals	420		$928.20	*172*	*$352.80*

Weighted-Average Method

Purchases			Total Cost
Date	Units	Unit Price	
January 1, beginning inventory	90	$2.00	*$180.00*
March 13, purchases	78	2.10	*163.80*
June 8, purchases	80	2.25	*180.00*
September 16, purchases	84	2.30	*193.20*
December 22, purchases	88	2.40	*211.20*
Totals	420		*$928.20*

Total of Beginning Inventory and Purchases	÷	*Total Units*	=	*Weighted-Average Price per Unit*
$928.20		*420*		*$2.21*

Units in Ending Inventory	×	*Weighted-Average Price per Unit*	=	*Cost of Ending Inventory*
172		*$2.21*		*$380.12*

19-3 APPLICATION PROBLEM, p. 579

Estimating ending inventory using the gross profit method

1.

STEP 1

Beginning inventory, March 1	$ 98,700.00
Plus net purchases for March 1 to March 31	+ 45,800.00
Equals cost of merchandise available for sale	$144,500.00

STEP 2

Net sales for March 1 to March 31	$186,000.00
Times previous year's gross profit percentage	× 58.0%
Equals estimated gross profit on operations	$107,880.00

STEP 3

Net sales for March 1 to March 31	$186,000.00
Less estimated gross profit on operations	−107,880.00
Equals estimated cost of merchandise sold	$ 78,120.00

STEP 4

Cost of merchandise available for sale	$144,500.00
Less estimated cost of merchandise sold	− 78,120.00
Equals estimated ending merchandise inventory	$ 66,380.00

2.

Fultz Industries

Income Statement

For Month Ended March 31, 20 – –

			% OF NET SALES
Operating Revenue:			
Net Sales		186,000.00	100.0
Cost of Merchandise Sold:			
Estimated Beginning Inventory, March 1	98,700.00		
Net Purchases	45,800.00		
Merchandise Available for Sale	144,500.00		
Less Estimated Ending Inventory, March 31	66,380.00		
Cost of Merchandise Sold		78,120.00	42.0
Gross Profit on Operations		107,880.00	58.0
Operating Expenses		80,352.00	43.2
Net Income		27,528.00	14.8

Name ______________________ Date ____________ Class ____________

19-4 MASTERY PROBLEM, p. 579

Determining the cost of inventory using the fifo, lifo, and weighted-average inventory costing methods

1.

STOCK RECORD

Description Electronic switch   Stock No. P-234

Reorder 20   Minimum 10   Location Aisle C-2

1	2	3	4	5	6	7
INCREASES			DECREASES			BALANCE
DATE	PURCHASE INVOICE NO.	QUANTITY	DATE	SALES INVOICE NO.	QUANTITY	QUANTITY
			Jan. 1		8	8
Jan. 6	*154*	*20*				*28*
			Apr. 5	*1998*	*22*	*6*
Apr. 14	*223*	*20*				*26*
			July 28	*2245*	*25*	*1*
Aug. 3	*298*	*20*				*21*
			Dec. 2	*2848*	*15*	*6*
Dec. 12	*332*	*20*				*26*

19-4 MASTERY PROBLEM (continued)

2.

FIFO Method

Purchase Dates	Units Purchased	Unit Price	Total Cost	FIFO Units on Hand	FIFO Cost
January 1, beginning inventory	8	$4.98	$ 39.84		
January 6, purchases	*20*	*5.12*	*102.40*		
April 14, purchases	*20*	*5.18*	*103.60*		
August 3, purchases	*20*	*5.23*	*104.60*	*6*	*$ 31.38*
December 12, purchases	*20*	*5.27*	*105.40*	*20*	*105.40*
Totals	*88*		*$455.84*	*26*	*$136.78*

LIFO Method

Purchase Dates	Units Purchased	Unit Price	Total Cost	LIFO Units on Hand	LIFO Cost
January 1, beginning inventory	8	$4.98	$ 39.84	*8*	*$ 39.84*
January 6, purchases	*20*	*5.12*	*102.40*	*18*	*92.16*
April 14, purchases	*20*	*5.18*	*103.60*		
August 3, purchases	*20*	*5.23*	*104.60*		
December 12, purchases	*20*	*5.27*	*105.40*		
Totals	*88*		*$455.84*	*26*	*$132.00*

Weighted-Average Method

Purchases			Total Cost
Date	Units	Unit Price	
January 1, beginning inventory	8	$4.98	$ 39.84
January 6, purchases	*20*	*5.12*	*102.40*
April 14, purchases	*20*	*5.18*	*103.60*
August 3, purchases	*20*	*5.23*	*104.60*
December 12, purchases	*20*	*5.27*	*105.40*
Totals	*88*		*$455.84*

Total of Beginning Inventory and Purchases	÷	Total Units	=	Weighted-Average Price per Unit
$455.84		*88*		*$5.18*

Units in Ending Inventory	×	Weighted-Average Price per Unit	=	Cost of Ending Inventory
26		*$5.18*		*$134.68*

Name ______________________ Date ______________ Class ______________

19-4 MASTERY PROBLEM (concluded)

3.

	Fifo	Lifo	Weighted-Average
Merchandise Available for Sale	*$455.84*	*$455.84*	*$455.84*
Ending Inventory	*136.78*	*132.00*	*134.68*
Cost of Merchandise Sold	*$319.06*	*$323.84*	*$321.16*

Highest Cost of Merchandise Sold: *lifo*

19-5 CHALLENGE PROBLEM, p. 580

Determining the cost of merchandise inventory destroyed in a fire

1.

Gross profit on operations	$323,899.40
Divided by net sales	÷645,217.90
Equals gross profit percentage of net sales (prior year)	50.2%

2.

STEP 1	
Beginning inventory, May 1	$ 34,543.98
Plus net purchases for May 1 to May 12	+ 6,754.03
Equals cost of merchandise available for sale	$ 41,298.01
STEP 2	
Net sales for May 1 to May 12	$ 22,432.87
Times previous year's gross profit percentage	× 50.2%
Equals estimated gross profit on operations	$ 11,261.30
STEP 3	
Net sales for May 1 to May 12	$ 22,432.87
Less estimated gross profit on operations	− 11,261.30
Equals estimated cost of merchandise sold	$ 11,171.57
STEP 4	
Cost of merchandise available for sale	$ 41,298.01
Less estimated cost of merchandise sold	− 11,171.57
Equals estimated ending merchandise inventory	$ 30,126.44

3.

Estimated merchandise inventory, May 12	$ 30,126.44
Less cost of merchandise inventory not destroyed	− 1,890.00
Equals estimated cost of merchandise inventory destroyed	$ 28,236.44

4.

Murphy Electronics Company

Income Statement

For the Period May 1 to May 12, 20 – –

			% OF NET SALES
Operating Revenue:			
Net Sales		22,432.87	100.0
Cost of Merchandise Sold:			
Estimated Beginning Inventory, May 1	34,543.98		
Net Purchases	6,754.03		
Merchandise Available for Sale	41,298.01		
Less Estimated Ending Inventory, May 12	30,126.44		
Cost of Merchandise Sold		11,171.57	49.8
Gross Profit on Operations		11,261.30	50.2
Operating Expenses		9,875.40	44.0
Net Income		1,385.90	6.2

Name ______________________ Date ____________ Class ____________

19-5 CHALLENGE PROBLEM (concluded)

5. *Book value of the inventory is the value shown on Murphy Electronics' financial records. Since Murphy Electronics does not maintain a perpetual inventory, the book value is the amount of estimated ending inventory on May 12.*

   Replacement value of the inventory is the amount Murphy Electronics would have to pay to replace the inventory at current prices.

6. *The fifo inventory costing method uses the most recent invoice prices to determine the cost of inventory on hand. Since the book value of the inventory is based on the most recent unit prices, the book value and replacement value of the inventory might be very similar.*

7. *The value the insurance company uses should be determined by the terms of the insurance policy. In most cases, a higher insurance premium is paid if replacement value is written into the policy.*

Study Guide 20

Name	Perfect Score	Your Score
Identifying Accounting Terms	18 Pts.	
Identifying Accounting Concepts and Practices	8 Pts.	
Analyzing Notes and Interest	8 Pts.	
Analyzing Notes Payable and Notes Receivable Transactions	14 Pts.	
Total	48 Pts.	

Part One—Identifying Accounting Terms

Directions: Select the one term in Column I that best fits each definition in Column II. Print the letter identifying your choice in the Answers column.

Column I	Column II	Answers
A. creditor	**1.** The number assigned to identify a specific note. (p. 589)	1. *N*
B. current liabilities	**2.** The date a note is signed. (p. 589)	2. *C*
C. date of a note	**3.** The person or business to whom the amount of a note is payable. (p. 589)	3. *O*
D. dishonored note	**4.** The days, months, or years from the date of signing until a note is to be paid. (p. 589)	4. *R*
E. interest	**5.** The original amount of a note. (p. 589)	5. *P*
F. interest expense	**6.** The percentage of the principal that is paid for use of the money. (p. 589)	6. *H*
G. interest income	**7.** The date a note is due. (p. 589)	7. *J*
H. interest rate of a note	**8.** The person or business who signs a note and thus promises to make payment. (p. 589)	8. *I*
I. maker of a note	**9.** A written and signed promise to pay a sum of money at a specified time. (p. 589)	9. *Q*
J. maturity date of a note	**10.** A person or organization to whom a liability is owed. (p. 589)	10. *A*
K. maturity value	**11.** Promissory notes signed by a business and given to a creditor. (p. 589)	11. *L*
L. notes payable	**12.** An amount paid for the use of money for a period of time. (p. 590)	12. *E*
M. notes receivable	**13.** The amount that is due on the maturity date of a note. (p. 590)	13. *K*
N. number of a note	**14.** Liabilities due within a short time, usually within a year. (p. 593)	14. *B*
O. payee of a note	**15.** The interest accrued on money borrowed. (p. 594)	15. *F*
P. principal of a note	**16.** Promissory notes that a business accepts from customers. (p. 598)	16. *M*
Q. promissory note	**17.** The interest earned on money loaned. (p. 599)	17. *G*
R. time of a note	**18.** A note that is not paid when due. (p. 600)	18. *D*

Part Two—Identifying Accounting Concepts and Practices

Directions: Place a *T* for True or an *F* for False in the Answers column to show whether each of the following statements is true or false.

	Answers
1. When the timing of cash receipts and required cash payments do not match, businesses usually deposit extra cash or borrow cash or make arrangements to delay payments. (p. 588)	1. *T*
2. "Interest at 12%" means that 12 cents will be paid for the use of each dollar borrowed for the time of a note. (p. 590)	2. *F*
3. An individual with a car loan usually pays the note in partial payments that include part of the principal and part of the interest on the note. (p. 590)	3. *T*
4. In interest calculations, time can be expressed in whole years or as a fraction of a year. (p. 590)	4. *T*
5. The maturity value of a note is calculated by subtracting the interest rate from the principal. (p. 590)	5. *F*
6. The journal entry for signing a note payable includes a debit to Interest Expense. (p. 593)	6. *F*
7. The journal entry for paying a note payable includes a debit to Accounts Payable to remove the balance owed. (p. 594)	7. *F*
8. When a note receivable is dishonored, the company should immediately write off the account receivable for that customer. (p. 600)	8. *F*

Part Three—Analyzing Notes and Interest

Directions: For each of the following items, select the choice that best completes the statement. Print the letter identifying your choice in the Answers column.

	Answers
1. The most useful evidence of a debt in a court of law is (A) an oral promise to pay (B) an account receivable (C) an account payable (D) a signed note (p. 589)	1. *D*
2. The interest on a 180-day, 10% interest-bearing note of $2,000.00 is (A) $20.00 (B) $200.00 (C) $100.00 (D) none of these (p. 590)	2. *C*
3. The time of a note issued for less than one year is typically stated in (A) days (B) months (C) a fraction of a year (D) none of these (p. 590)	3. *A*
4. The maturity value of a 90-day, 12% interest-bearing note of $600.00 is (A) $582.00 (B) $672.00 (C) $624.00 (D) none of these (p. 590)	4. *D*
5. The maturity date of a 90-day note dated August 22 is (A) November 19 (B) November 20 (C) November 21 (D) November 22 (p. 591)	5. *B*
6. Notes payable are classified as (A) current assets (B) current liabilities (C) expenses (D) revenue (p. 593)	6. *B*
7. The source document for recording cash received from signing a note payable is a (A) receipt (B) check (C) memorandum (D) copy of the note (p. 593)	7. *A*
8. Notes receivable are classified as (A) other expense (B) current assets (C) current liabilities (D) other revenue (p. 598)	8. *B*

Name ______________________ Date ______________ Class ______________

Part Four—Analyzing Notes Payable and Notes Receivable Transactions

Directions: Analyze each of the following transactions into debit and credit parts. Print the letter identifying your choices in the proper Answers column.

Account Titles

A. Accounts Payable
B. Accounts Receivable
C. Cash
D. Interest Expense
E. Interest Income
F. Notes Payable
G. Notes Receivable

ACCTS. RECEIVABLE LEDGER

H. Aimee Kane
I. Common Grounds Coffee Shop

ACCTS. PAYABLE LEDGER

J. Café on the Way

Transactions	Answers Debit	Answers Credit
1–2. Signed a 90-day, 10% note. (p. 593)	1. *C*	2. *F*
3–4. Paid cash for the maturity value of a note plus interest. (p. 594)	3. *D, F*	4. *C*
5–6. Signed a 60-day, 18% note to Café on the Way for an extension of time on an account payable. (p. 595)	5. *A, J*	6. *F*
7–8. Paid cash for the maturity value of the note payable to Café on the Way. (p. 596)	7. *D, F*	8. *C*
9–10. Accepted a 90-day, 18% note from Aimee Kane for an extension of time on her account. (p. 598)	9. *G*	10. *B, H*
11–12. Received cash for the maturity value of the note receivable plus interest from Aimee Kane. (p. 599)	11. *C*	12. *E, G*
13–14. Common Grounds Coffee Shop dishonored a note receivable, maturity value due today. (p. 600)	13. *B, I*	14. *E, G*

Name ______________________ Date ____________ Class ____________

20-1 WORK TOGETHER, p. 592

Calculating interest, maturity dates, and maturity values for promissory notes

Date	Principal	Interest Rate	Time	Interest	Maturity Date	Maturity Value
March 3	$6,000.00	6%	90 days	*$90.00*	*June 1*	*$6,090.00*
March 18	$2,000.00	9%	60 days	*$30.00*	*May 17*	*$2,030.00*

Calculations:

Date of Note	*Interest*	*Maturity Date*		*Maturity Value*
March 3	*$6,000 × 6% × 90/360 = $90*	*March 3–31* *April* *May* *June 1* *Total*	*28 days* *30 days* *31 days* *1 day* *90 days*	*$6,000 + $90 = $6,090*
March 18	*$2,000 × 9% × 60/360 = $30*	*March 18–31* *April* *May 1–17* *Total*	*13 days* *30 days* *17 days* *60 days*	*$2,000 + $30 = $2,030*

20-1 ON YOUR OWN, p. 592

Calculating interest, maturity dates, and maturity values for promissory notes

Date	Principal	Interest Rate	Time	Interest	Maturity Date	Maturity Value
June 8	$20,000.00	8%	180 days	***$800.00***	***Dec. 5***	***$20,800.00***
June 12	$10,000.00	6%	90 days	***$150.00***	***Sept. 10***	***$10,150.00***

Calculations:

Date of Note	*Interest*	*Maturity Date*		*Maturity Value*
June 8	*$20,000 × 8% × 180/360 = $800*	*June 8–30* *July* *August* *September* *October* *November* *December* *Total*	*22 days* *31 days* *31 days* *30 days* *31 days* *30 days* *5 days* *180 days*	*$20,000 + $800 = $20,800*
June 12	*$10,000 × 6% × 90/360 = $150*	*June 12–30* *July* *August* *September 1–10* *Total*	*18 days* *31 days* *31 days* *10 days* *90 days*	*$10,000 + $150 = $10,150*

Name ________________ Date ________ Class ________

20-2 WORK TOGETHER, p. 597

Journalizing notes payable transactions

1.

GENERAL JOURNAL — PAGE 3

	DATE		ACCOUNT TITLE	DOC. NO.	POST. REF.	DEBIT	CREDIT	
1	20-- Mar.	18	Accounts Payable/DryCreek Company	M288	/	2 000 00		1
2			Notes Payable				2 000 00	2
3								3
4								4

1.

CASH RECEIPTS JOURNAL — PAGE 5

	DATE		ACCOUNT TITLE	DOC. NO.	POST. REF.	1 GENERAL DEBIT	2 GENERAL CREDIT	3 ACCOUNTS RECEIVABLE CREDIT	4 SALES CREDIT	5 SALES TAX PAYABLE CREDIT	6 SALES DISCOUNT DEBIT	7 CASH DEBIT	
1	20-- Mar.	3	Notes Payable	R279			6 000 00					6 000 00	1
2													2
3													3
4													4
5													5

2.

CASH PAYMENTS JOURNAL — PAGE 9

	DATE		ACCOUNT TITLE	CK. NO.	POST. REF.	1 GENERAL DEBIT	2 GENERAL CREDIT	3 ACCOUNTS PAYABLE DEBIT	4 PURCHASES DISCOUNT CREDIT	5 CASH CREDIT	
1	20-- May	17	Notes Payable	255		2 000 00				2 030 00	1
2			Interest Expense			30 00					2
3	June	1	Notes Payable	263		6 000 00				6 090 00	3
4			Interest Expense			90 00					4
5											5

Journalizing notes payable transactions

1.

GENERAL JOURNAL — PAGE 10

	DATE		ACCOUNT TITLE	DOC. NO.	POST. REF.	DEBIT	CREDIT	
1	20-- June	12	Accounts Payable/Best Company	M165	/	10 000 00		1
2			Notes Payable				10 000 00	2
3								3
4								4

1.

CASH RECEIPTS JOURNAL — PAGE 20

	DATE		ACCOUNT TITLE	DOC. NO.	POST. REF.	1 GENERAL DEBIT	2 GENERAL CREDIT	3 ACCOUNTS RECEIVABLE CREDIT	4 SALES CREDIT	5 SALES TAX PAYABLE CREDIT	6 SALES DISCOUNT DEBIT	7 CASH DEBIT	
1	20-- June	8	Notes Payable	R361			20 000 00					20 000 00	1
2													2
3													3
4													4
5													5

2.

CASH PAYMENTS JOURNAL — PAGE 17

	DATE		ACCOUNT TITLE	CK. NO.	POST. REF.	1 GENERAL DEBIT	2 GENERAL CREDIT	3 ACCOUNTS PAYABLE DEBIT	4 PURCHASES DISCOUNT CREDIT	5 CASH CREDIT	
1	20-- Sept.	10	Notes Payable	601		10 000 00				10 150 00	1
2			Interest Expense			150 00					2
3	Dec.	5	Notes Payable	882		20 000 00				20 800 00	3
4			Interest Expense			800 00					4
5											5

Name ______________________ Date ______________ Class ______________

20-3 WORK TOGETHER, p. 602

Journalizing notes receivable transactions

GENERAL JOURNAL — PAGE 2

	DATE		ACCOUNT TITLE	DOC. NO.	POST. REF.	DEBIT	CREDIT	
1	20-- Feb.	2	Notes Receivable	NR17		1 800 00		1
2			Accounts Receivable/Paul Gary		/		1 800 00	2
3		27	Accounts Receivable/Kirk Adams	M25	/	409 00		3
4			Notes Receivable				400 00	4
5			Interest Income				9 00	5
6								6

CASH RECEIPTS JOURNAL — PAGE 3

	DATE		ACCOUNT TITLE	DOC. NO.	POST. REF.	1 GENERAL DEBIT	2 GENERAL CREDIT	3 ACCOUNTS RECEIVABLE CREDIT	4 SALES CREDIT	5 SALES TAX PAYABLE CREDIT	6 SALES DISCOUNT DEBIT	7 CASH DEBIT	
1	20-- Feb.	18	Notes Receivable	R67			500 00					507 50	1
2			Interest Income				7 50						2
3													3
4													4
5													5

20-3 ON YOUR OWN, p. 602

Journalizing notes receivable transactions

GENERAL JOURNAL — PAGE 3

	DATE		ACCOUNT TITLE	DOC. NO.	POST. REF.	DEBIT	CREDIT	
1	20-- Mar.	4	Notes Receivable	NR24		2,500.00		1
2			Accounts Receivable/Kim Pratt		✓		2,500.00	2
3		26	Accounts Receivable/T. J. Cross	M21	✓	1,845.00		3
4			Notes Receivable				1,800.00	4
5			Interest Income				45.00	5
6								6

CASH RECEIPTS JOURNAL — PAGE 5

	DATE		ACCOUNT TITLE	DOC. NO.	POST. REF.	1 GENERAL DEBIT	2 GENERAL CREDIT	3 ACCOUNTS RECEIVABLE CREDIT	4 SALES CREDIT	5 SALES TAX PAYABLE CREDIT	6 SALES DISCOUNT DEBIT	7 CASH DEBIT	
1	20-- Mar.	18	Notes Receivable	R68			1,500.00					1,530.00	1
2			Interest Income				30.00						2
3													3
4													4
5													5

Name ______________________ Date ______________ Class ______________

20-1 APPLICATION PROBLEM, p. 604

Calculating interest, maturity dates, and maturity values for promissory notes

Date	Principal	Interest Rate	Time	Interest	Maturity Date	Maturity Value
April 6	$10,000.00	12%	180 days	*$600.00*	*Oct. 3*	*$10,600.00*
April 12	$600.00	9%	60 days	*$9.00*	*June 11*	*$609.00*
April 15	$5,000.00	10%	90 days	*$125.00*	*July 14*	*$5,125.00*
April 23	$3,000.00	14%	60 days	*$70.00*	*June 22*	*$3,070.00*

Calculations:

Date of Note	*Interest*	*Maturity Date*		*Maturity Value*
April 6	*$10,000 × 12% × 180/360 = $600*	*April 6–30* *May* *June* *July* *August* *September* *October 1–3* *Total*	*24 days* *31 days* *30 days* *31 days* *31 days* *30 days* *3 days* *180 days*	*$10,000 + $600 = $10,600*
April 12	*$600 × 9% × 60/360 = $9*	*April 12–30* *May* *June 1–11* *Total*	*18 days* *31 days* *11 days* *60 days*	*$600 + $9 = $609*
April 15	*$5,000 × 10% × 90/360 = $125*	*April 15–30* *May* *June* *July 1–14* *Total*	*15 days* *31 days* *30 days* *14 days* *90 days*	*$5,000 + $125 = $5,125*
April 23	*$3,000 × 14% × 60/360 = $70*	*April 23–30* *May* *June 1–22* *Total*	*7 days* *31 days* *22 days* *60 days*	*$3,000 + $70 = $3,070*

Journalizing notes payable transactions

1.

GENERAL JOURNAL — PAGE 4

	DATE		ACCOUNT TITLE	DOC. NO.	POST. REF.	DEBIT	CREDIT	
1	20-- Apr.	12	Accounts Payable/Milligan Company	M32	/	600 00		1
2			Notes Payable				600 00	2
3		23	Accounts Payable/Yeatman Industries	M42	/	3000 00		3
4			Notes Payable				3000 00	4
5								5
6								6

CASH RECEIPTS JOURNAL — PAGE 6

	DATE		ACCOUNT TITLE	DOC. NO.	POST. REF.	1 GENERAL DEBIT	2 GENERAL CREDIT	3 ACCOUNTS RECEIVABLE CREDIT	4 SALES CREDIT	5 SALES TAX PAYABLE CREDIT	6 SALES DISCOUNT DEBIT	7 CASH DEBIT	
1	20-- Apr.	6	Notes Payable	R127			10000 00					10000 00	1
2		15	Notes Payable	R142			5000 00					5000 00	2
3													3
4													4
5													5
6													6
7													7
8													8
9													9
10													10

Name ______________________ Date ______________ Class ______________

20-2 APPLICATION PROBLEM (concluded)

2.

CASH PAYMENTS JOURNAL

PAGE 9

	DATE		ACCOUNT TITLE	CK. NO.	POST. REF.	GENERAL DEBIT (1)	GENERAL CREDIT (2)	ACCOUNTS PAYABLE DEBIT (3)	PURCHASES DISCOUNT CREDIT (4)	CASH CREDIT (5)	
1	20-- June	11	Notes Payable	310		600 00				609 00	1
2			Interest Expense			9 00					2
3		22	Notes Payable	318		3 000 00				3 070 00	3
4			Interest Expense			70 00					4
5	July	14	Notes Payable	456		5 000 00				5 125 00	5
6			Interest Expense			125 00					6
7	Oct.	3	Notes Payable	645		10 000 00				10 600 00	7
8			Interest Expense			600 00					8
9											9
10											10
11											11
12											12
13											13
14											14
15											15
16											16
17											17
18											18
19											19
20											20
21											21
22											22
23											23
24											24

20-3 APPLICATION PROBLEM, p. 605

Journalizing notes receivable transactions

GENERAL JOURNAL PAGE 14

DATE		ACCOUNT TITLE	DOC. NO.	POST. REF.	DEBIT	CREDIT
20-- July	5	Notes Receivable	NR25		3000 00	
		Accounts Receivable/Peter Lamb				3000 00
	15	Notes Receivable	NR26		2400 00	
		Accounts Receivable/Pam Sellers				2400 00
	21	Accounts Receivable/Josh Kemp	M62		3605 00	
		Notes Receivable				3500 00
		Interest Income				105 00
	27	Accounts Receivable/Phil Pellum	M63		2593 75	
		Notes Receivable				2500 00
		Interest Income				93 75

Name ______________________ Date ______________ Class ______________

20-3 APPLICATION PROBLEM (concluded)

CASH RECEIPTS JOURNAL

PAGE 10

	DATE	ACCOUNT TITLE	DOC. NO.	POST. REF.	1 GENERAL DEBIT	2 GENERAL CREDIT	3 ACCOUNTS RECEIVABLE CREDIT	4 SALES CREDIT	5 SALES TAX PAYABLE CREDIT	6 SALES DISCOUNT DEBIT	7 CASH DEBIT	
1	20-- July 11	Notes Receivable	R321			800 00					812 00	1
2		Interest Income				12 00						2
3	22	Notes Receivable	R339			1000 00					1025 00	3
4		Interest Income				25 00						4
5												5
6												6
7												7
8												8
9												9
10												10
11												11
12												12
13												13
14												14
15												15
16												16
17												17
18												18
19												19
20												20
21												21
22												22
23												23
24												24
25												25

20-4 APPLICATION PROBLEM, p. 605

Journalizing notes receivable transactions

GENERAL JOURNAL PAGE 18

	DATE		ACCOUNT TITLE	DOC. NO.	POST. REF.	DEBIT	CREDIT	
1	20-- Nov.	3	Notes Receivable	NR63		3 000 00		1
2			Accounts Receivable/AutoCare Industries				3 000 00	2
3		28	Accounts Receivable/Sanford Company	M69		4 180 00		3
4			Notes Receivable				4 000 00	4
5			Interest Income				180 00	5
6								6
7								7
8								8
9								9
10								10
11								11
12								12
13								13
14								14
15								15
16								16
17								17
18								18
19								19
20								20
21								21
22								22
23								23
24								24
25								25
26								26
27								27
28								28
29								29
30								30
31								31
32								32
33								33

20-4 APPLICATION PROBLEM (concluded)

CASH RECEIPTS JOURNAL

PAGE 11

	DATE	ACCOUNT TITLE	DOC. NO.	POST. REF.	1 GENERAL DEBIT	2 GENERAL CREDIT	3 ACCOUNTS RECEIVABLE CREDIT	4 SALES CREDIT	5 SALES TAX PAYABLE CREDIT	6 SALES DISCOUNT DEBIT	7 CASH DEBIT	
1	20-- Nov. 14	Notes Receivable	R245			2 000 00					2 090 00	1
2		Interest Income				90 00						2
3												3
4												4
5												5
6												6
7												7
8												8
9												9
10												10
11												11
12												12
13												13
14												14
15												15
16												16
17												17
18												18
19												19
20												20
21												21
22												22
23												23
24												24
25												25

20-5 MASTERY PROBLEM, p. 606

Journalizing notes payable and notes receivable transactions

1.

GENERAL JOURNAL

PAGE 7

	DATE		ACCOUNT TITLE	DOC. NO.	POST. REF.	DEBIT	CREDIT	
1	20-- July	7	Notes Receivable	NR9		1,500.00		1
2			Accounts Receivable/Nan Abert		✓		1,500.00	2
3		12	Notes Receivable	NR10		400.00		3
4			Accounts Receivable/Tom Burns		✓		400.00	4
5		24	Accounts Receivable/Gibson Co.	M43	✓	3,090.00		5
6			Notes Receivable				3,000.00	6
7			Interest Income				90.00	7
8		29	Accounts Payable/Daily Supply	M44	✓	2,500.00		8
9			Notes Payable				2,500.00	9

CASH RECEIPTS JOURNAL

PAGE 6

	DATE		ACCOUNT TITLE	DOC. NO.	POST. REF.	1 GENERAL DEBIT	2 GENERAL CREDIT	3 ACCOUNTS RECEIVABLE CREDIT	4 SALES CREDIT	5 SALES TAX PAYABLE CREDIT	6 SALES DISCOUNT DEBIT	7 CASH DEBIT	
1	20-- July	2	Notes Payable	R51			5,000.00					5,000.00	1
2		9	Notes Receivable	R62			1,600.00					1,624.00	2
3			Interest Income				24.00						3
4		17	Notes Receivable	R65			800.00					812.00	4
5			Interest Income				12.00						5
6		23	Notes Payable	R74			8,000.00					8,000.00	6
7		28	Notes Receivable	R79			4,500.00					4,635.00	7
8			Interest Income				135.00						8
9													9

Name ______________________ Date ____________ Class ____________

20-5 MASTERY PROBLEM (continued)

2.

Calculations:

July 2, 90-Day Note:

Maturity Date:		*Maturity Value:*
July 2–31	*29 days*	*$5,000 × 10% × 90/360 = $125*
August	*31 days*	
September	*30 days*	*$5,000 + $125 = $5,125*
Total	*90 days*	

July 23, 180-Day Note:

Maturity Date:		*Maturity Value:*
July 23–31	*8 days*	*$8,000 × 8% × 180/360 = $320*
August	*31 days*	
September	*30 days*	*$8,000 + $320 = $8,320*
October	*31 days*	
November	*30 days*	
December	*31 days*	
January 1–19	*19 days*	
Total	*180 days*	

July 29, 60-Day Note:

Maturity Date:		*Maturity Value:*
July 29–31	*2 days*	*$2,500 × 12% × 60/360 = $50*
August	*31 days*	
September 1–27	*27 days*	*$2,500 + $50 = $2,550*
Total	*60 days*	

20-5 MASTERY PROBLEM (concluded)

3.

CASH PAYMENTS JOURNAL

PAGE 9

	DATE		ACCOUNT TITLE	CK. NO.	POST. REF.	1 GENERAL DEBIT	2 GENERAL CREDIT	3 ACCOUNTS PAYABLE DEBIT	4 PURCHASES DISCOUNT CREDIT	5 CASH CREDIT	
1	20-- Sept.	27	Notes Payable	417		2,500.00				2,550.00	1
2			Interest Expense			50.00					2
3	Sept.	30	Notes Payable	610		5,000.00				5,125.00	3
4			Interest Expense			125.00					4
5	Jan.	19	Notes Payable	821		8,000.00				8,320.00	5
6			Interest Expense			320.00					6
7											7
8											8
9											9
10											10
11											11
12											12
13											13
14											14
15											15
16											16
17											17
18											18
19											19
20											20
21											21
22											22
23											23
24											24

Name ______________________ Date ____________ Class ____________

20-6 CHALLENGE PROBLEM, p. 606

Recording notes receivable stated in months

1.

June 18–30	*12 days*
July	*31 days*
August	*31 days*
September 1–18	*18 days*
Total	*92 days*

Maturity Value:

$10,000.00 × 15% × 92/360 = $383.33

$10,000.00 + $383.33 = $10,383.33

2.

Maturity Value:

$10,000.00 × 15% × 90/360 = $375.00

$10,000.00 + $375.00 = $10,375.00

3.

Actual Interest Rate:

$10,000.00 × Interest Rate × 92/360 = $375.00 Interest

Interest Rate × 92/360 = $375.00/$10,000.00

Interest Rate × 92/360 = .0375

Interest Rate = .0375 × 360/92

= 14.67%

4.

The bank must weigh the short-term cost of losing $8.33 ($383.33 – $375.00) of interest income against the potential long-term cost of losing a long-time customer of the bank. Initially, it would seem reasonable to allow Mr. Whiley to have the reduced actual interest rate of 14.67% since the cost is very small on this loan. However, the bank must also consider its ability to negotiate future loans with other bank customers.

Name ______________________ Date ____________ Class ____________

REINFORCEMENT ACTIVITY 3 PART A, pp. 610–613

An accounting cycle for a corporation: journalizing and posting transactions

1.

GENERAL JOURNAL PAGE 12

DATE		ACCOUNT TITLE	DOC. NO.	POST. REF.	DEBIT	CREDIT
20-- Dec.	6	*Supplies*	*M45*	*1140*	*362 40*	
		Accounts Payable/Draper Company		*2115/220*		*362 40*
	7	*Notes Receivable*	*NR34*	*1115*	*3 600 00*	
		Accounts Receivable/Nelson Co.		*1125/150*		*3 600 00*
	9	*Allowance for Uncollectible Accounts*	*M46*	*1130*	*2 460 00*	
		Accounts Receivable/Felton Industries		*1125/120*		*2 460 00*
	14	*Depreciation Expense—Warehouse Equipment*	*M47*	*6125*	*440 00*	
		Accumulated Depreciation—Warehouse Equip.		*1220*		*440 00*
	14	*Accounts Payable/Glenson Company*	*DM34*	*2115/230*	*198 00*	
		Purchases Returns and Allowances		*5115*		*198 00*
	15	*Payroll Taxes Expense*	*M48*	*6140*	*250 45*	
		Social Security Tax Payable		*2130*		*174 84*
		Medicare Tax Payable		*2135*		*40 89*
		Unemployment Tax Payable—Federal		*2145*		*4 48*
		Unemployment Tax Payable—State		*2150*		*30 24*
	18	*Accounts Receivable/Baker & Associates*	*M49*	*1125/110*	*948 00*	
		Allowance for Uncollectible Accounts		*1130*		*948 00*
	22	*Sales Returns and Allowances*	*CM15*	*4115*	*120 00*	
		Sales Tax Payable		*2140*	*7 20*	
		Accounts Receivable/Ruocco Plastics		*1125/160*		*127 20*
	28	*Depreciation Expense—Office Equipment*	*M50*	*6120*	*240 00*	
		Accumulated Depreciation—Office Equipment		*1210*		*240 00*
	30	*Accounts Receivable/Ruocco Plastics*	*M51*	*1125/160*	*3 060 00*	
		Notes Receivable		*1115*		*3 000 00*
		Interest Income		*7110*		*60 00*
	31	*Payroll Taxes Expense*	*M53*	*6140*	*242 14*	
		Social Security Tax Payable		*2130*		*171 12*
		Medicare Tax Payable		*2135*		*40 02*
		Unemployment Tax Payable—Federal		*2145*		*4 00*
		Unemployment Tax Payable—State		*2150*		*27 00*

REINFORCEMENT ACTIVITY 3 PART A (continued)

1., 2.

SALES JOURNAL PAGE 12

DATE		ACCOUNT DEBITED	SALE NO.	POST. REF.	1 ACCOUNTS RECEIVABLE DEBIT	2 SALES CREDIT	3 SALES TAX PAYABLE CREDIT
20-- Dec.	5	*Horton Company*	657	140	530 00	500 00	30 00
	9	*Ruocco Plastics*	658	160	508 80	480 00	28 80
	20	*Hilldale School*	659	130	1 560 00	1 560 00	
	28	*Horton Company*	660	140	2 650 00	2 500 00	150 00
	31	*Totals*			5 248 80	5 040 00	208 80
					(1125)	(4105)	(2140)

Name ______________________ Date ____________ Class ____________

REINFORCEMENT ACTIVITY 3 PART A (continued)

1., 3.

PURCHASES JOURNAL — PAGE 12

	DATE		ACCOUNT CREDITED	PURCH. NO.	POST. REF.	PURCHASES DR. ACCTS. PAY. CR.	
1	20-- Dec.	8	*Glenson Company*	332	230	4,518 00	1
2		12	*Hinsdale Supply Co.*	333	240	6,812 00	2
3		16	*Buntin Supply Company*	334	210	4,833 00	3
4		28	*Draper Company*	335	220	6,148 00	4
5		31	*Total*			22,311 00	5
6						(5105)(2115)	6

1., 4., 6.

CASH RECEIPTS JOURNAL PAGE 12

	DATE		ACCOUNT TITLE	DOC. NO.	POST. REF.	1 GENERAL DEBIT	2 GENERAL CREDIT	3 ACCOUNTS RECEIVABLE CREDIT	4 SALES CREDIT	5 SALES TAX PAYABLE CREDIT	6 SALES DISCOUNT DEBIT	7 CASH DEBIT	
1	20-- Dec.	2	Ruocco Plastics	R671	160			3250 00				3250 00	1
2		6	✔	TS49	✔				5430 00	325 80		5755 80	2
3		12	Horton Company	R672	140			530 00			10 60	519 40	3
4		13	✔	TS50	✔				5987 00	359 22		6346 22	4
5		14	Acc. Dep.—Warehouse Eq.	R673	1220	1880 00						1400 00	5
6			Warehouse Equipment		1215		2900 00						6
7			Gain on Plant Assets		7105		380 00						7
8		18	Baker & Associates	R674	110			948 00				948 00	8
9		20	✔	TS51	✔				3554 00	213 24		3767 24	9
10		26	Notes Receivable	R675	1115		5800 00					5974 00	10
11			Interest Income		7110		174 00						11
12		27	✔	TS52	✔				2337 00	140 22		2477 22	12
13		28	Notes Payable	R676	2105		6000 00					6000 00	13
14		28	Acc. Dep.—Office Equip.	R677	1210	660 00						150 00	14
15			Loss on Plant Assets		8110	40 00							15
16			Office Equipment		1205		850 00						16
17		31	✔	TS53	✔				465 00	27 90		492 90	17
18		31	Totals			2580 00	16104 00	4728 00	17773 00	1066 38	10 60	37080 78	18
19						(✔)	(✔)	(1125)	(4105)	(2140)	(4110)	(1105)	19

5.

CASH PROOF

Cash on hand at the beginning of the month	$ 3,959.80
Plus total cash received during the month	37,080.78
Equals total	$41,040.58
Less total cash paid during the month	32,939.88
Equals cash balance on hand at end of the month	$ 8,100.70
Checkbook balance on the next unused check stub	$ 8,100.70

Name ______________________ Date ______________ Class ______________

REINFORCEMENT ACTIVITY 3 PART A (continued)

1., 4., 7.

CASH PAYMENTS JOURNAL — PAGE 23

	DATE 20--		ACCOUNT TITLE	CK. NO.	POST. REF.	1 GENERAL DEBIT	2 GENERAL CREDIT	3 ACCOUNTS PAYABLE DEBIT	4 PURCHASES DISCOUNT CREDIT	5 CASH CREDIT	
1	Dec.	1	*Rent Expense*	578	6145	1,750.00				1,750.00	1
2		3	*Walbash Manufacturing*	579	260			620.00	12.40	607.60	2
3		3	*Notes Payable*	580	2105	10,000.00				10,450.00	3
4			*Interest Expense*		8105	450.00					4
5		5	*Office Equipment*	581	1205	1,200.00				1,200.00	5
6		10	*Supplies*	582	1140	223.00				223.00	6
7		15	*Employee Income Tax Payable*	583	2125	324.00				1,228.35	7
8			*Social Security Tax Payable*		2130	742.00					8
9			*Medicare Tax Payable*		2135	162.35					9
10		15	*Salary Expense*	584	6155	2,820.00				2,256.27	10
11			*Employee Income Tax Payable*		2125		158.00				11
12			*Social Security Tax Payable*		2130		174.84				12
13			*Medicare Tax Payable*		2135		40.89				13
14			*Health Insurance Premiums Payable*		2155		190.00				14
15		17	*Utilities Expense*	585	6170	346.20				346.20	15
16		17	*Accounts Payable/Glenson Co.*	586	230			4,518.00	90.36	4,427.64	16
17		19	*Miscellaneous Expense*	587	6135	72.00				72.00	17
18		21	*Purchases*	588	5105	357.00				357.00	18
19		23	*Hinsdale Supply Co.*	589	240			6,812.00		6,812.00	19
20		29	*SHF Corp.*	590	250			500.00		500.00	20
21		30	*Credit Card Fee Expense*	M52	6115	418.00				418.00	21
22		31	*Supplies*	591	1140	12.50				84.96	22
23			*Advertising Expense*		6105	50.00					23
24			*Miscellaneous Expense*		6135	22.37					24
25			*Cash Short and Over*		6110	0.09					25
26		31	*Salary Expense*	592	6155	2,760.00				2,206.86	26
27			*Employee Income Tax Payable*		2125		152.00				27
28			*Social Security Tax Payable*		2130		171.12				28
29			*Medicare Tax Payable*		2135		40.02				29
30			*Health Insurance Premiums Payable*		2155		190.00				30
31		31	*Totals*			21,709.51	1,116.87	12,450.00	102.76	32,939.88	31
32						(✔)	(✔)	(2115)	(5110)	(1105)	32

REINFORCEMENT ACTIVITY 3 PART A (continued)

1., 9.

PLANT ASSET RECORD No. 432 — General Ledger Account No. 1215

Description: Hand Truck — General Ledger Account: Warehouse Equip.

Date Bought: January 5, 20X1 — Serial Number: 215-225 — Original Cost: $2,900.00

Estimated Useful Life: 5 years — Estimated Salvage Value: $500.00 — Depreciation Method: Straight-line

Disposed of: Discarded ______ Sold ✔ Traded ______

Date: *December 14, 20X4* — Disposal Amount: ***$1,400.00***

Year	Annual Depreciation Expense	Accumulated Depreciation	Ending Book Value
20X1	$480.00	$ 480.00	$2,420.00
20X2	480.00	960.00	1,940.00
20X3	480.00	1,440.00	1,460.00
20X4	***440.00***	***1,880.00***	***1,020.00***

PLANT ASSET RECORD No. 667 — General Ledger Account No. 1205

Description: Computer Printer — General Ledger Account: Office Equipment

Date Bought: April 5, 20X1 — Serial Number: BE35CC — Original Cost: $850.00

Estimated Useful Life: 3 years — Estimated Salvage Value: $130.00 — Depreciation Method: Straight-line

Disposed of: Discarded ______ Sold ✔ Traded ______

Date: *December 28, 20X4* — Disposal Amount: ***$150.00***

Year	Annual Depreciation Expense	Accumulated Depreciation	Ending Book Value
20X2	$180.00	$180.00	$670.00
20X3	240.00	420.00	430.00
20X4	***240.00***	***660.00***	***190.00***

REINFORCEMENT ACTIVITY 3 PART A (continued)

PLANT ASSET RECORD No. *998* General Ledger Account No. *1205*

Description *Printer/Scanner* General Ledger Account *Office Equipment*

Date Bought *December 5, 20X4* Serial Number *MNT-9343* Original Cost *$1,200.00*

Estimated Useful Life *3 years* Estimated Salvage Value *$200.00* Depreciation Method *Straight-line*

Disposed of: Discarded ______ Sold ______ Traded ______

Date ______ Disposal Amount ______

Year	Annual Depreciation Expense	Accumulated Depreciation	Ending Book Value
20X4	$27.78	$27.78	$1,172.22

REINFORCEMENT ACTIVITY 3 PART A (continued)

1.

ACCOUNTS RECEIVABLE LEDGER

CUSTOMER Baker & Associates — CUSTOMER NO. 110

DATE		ITEM	POST. REF.	DEBIT	CREDIT	DEBIT BALANCE
20-- Dec.	18	Reopen account	G12	948 00		948 00
	18		CR12		948 00	—

CUSTOMER Felton Industries — CUSTOMER NO. 120

DATE		ITEM	POST. REF.	DEBIT	CREDIT	DEBIT BALANCE
20-- Dec.	1	Balance	✔			2,460 00
	9	Written off	G12		2,460 00	—

CUSTOMER Hilldale School — CUSTOMER NO. 130

DATE		ITEM	POST. REF.	DEBIT	CREDIT	DEBIT BALANCE
20-- Dec.	1	Balance	✔			243 00
	20		S12	1,560 00		1,803 00

CUSTOMER Horton Company — CUSTOMER NO. 140

DATE		ITEM	POST. REF.	DEBIT	CREDIT	DEBIT BALANCE
20-- Dec.	5		S12	530 00		530 00
	12		CR12		530 00	—
	28		S12	2,650 00		2,650 00

CUSTOMER Nelson Co. — CUSTOMER NO. 150

DATE		ITEM	POST. REF.	DEBIT	CREDIT	DEBIT BALANCE
20-- Dec.	1	Balance	✔			3,600 00
	7	Accepted note receivable	G12		3,600 00	—

REINFORCEMENT ACTIVITY 3 PART A (continued)

CUSTOMER Ruocco Plastics CUSTOMER NO. 160

DATE		ITEM	POST. REF.	DEBIT	CREDIT	DEBIT BALANCE
20-- Dec.	1	Balance	✓			3,250.00
	2		CR12		3,250.00	—
	9		S12	508.80		508.80
	22		G12		127.20	381.60
	30	Dishonored note receivable	G12	3,060.00		3,441.60

8.

Sparkle, Inc.

Schedule of Accounts Receivable

December 31, 20 – –

Hilldale School	1,803.00
Horton Company	2,650.00
Ruocco Plastics	3,441.60
Total Accounts Receivable	7,894.60

REINFORCEMENT ACTIVITY 3 PART A (continued)

1.

ACCOUNTS PAYABLE LEDGER

VENDOR Buntin Supply Company — VENDOR NO. 210

DATE		ITEM	POST. REF.	DEBIT	CREDIT	CREDIT BALANCE
20-- Dec.	1	Balance	✔			1 272 00
	16		P12		4 833 00	6 105 00

VENDOR Draper Company — VENDOR NO. 220

DATE		ITEM	POST. REF.	DEBIT	CREDIT	CREDIT BALANCE
20-- Dec.	1	Balance	✔			1 417 25
	6		G12		362 40	1 779 65
	28		P12		6 148 00	7 927 65

VENDOR Glenson Company — VENDOR NO. 230

DATE		ITEM	POST. REF.	DEBIT	CREDIT	CREDIT BALANCE
20-- Dec.	1	Balance	✔			198 00
	8		P12		4 518 00	4 716 00
	14		G12	198 00		4 518 00
	17		CP23	4 518 00		—

VENDOR Hinsdale Supply Co. — VENDOR NO. 240

DATE		ITEM	POST. REF.	DEBIT	CREDIT	CREDIT BALANCE
20-- Dec.	12		P12		6 812 00	6 812 00
	23		CP23	6 812 00		—

VENDOR SHF Corp. — VENDOR NO. 250

DATE		ITEM	POST. REF.	DEBIT	CREDIT	CREDIT BALANCE
20-- Dec.	1	Balance	✔			580 00
	29		CP23	500 00		80 00

REINFORCEMENT ACTIVITY 3 PART A (continued)

VENDOR Walbash Manufacturing VENDOR NO. 260

DATE		ITEM	POST. REF.	DEBIT	CREDIT	CREDIT BALANCE
20-- Dec.	1	Balance	✔			6 2 0 00
	3		CP23	6 2 0 00		—

8.

Sparkle, Inc.

Schedule of Accounts Payable

December 31, 20 – –

Buntin Supply Company	6 1 0 5 00
Draper Company	7 9 2 7 65
SHF Corp.	8 0 00
Total Accounts Payable	14 1 1 2 65

REINFORCEMENT ACTIVITY 3 PART A (continued)

1., 2., 3., 6., 7., 18., 19., 21.

GENERAL LEDGER

ACCOUNT Cash — ACCOUNT NO. 1105

DATE 20--		ITEM	POST. REF.	DEBIT	CREDIT	BALANCE DEBIT	BALANCE CREDIT
Dec.	1	Balance	✔			3,959.80	
	31		CR12	37,080.78		41,040.58	
	31		CP23		32,939.88	8,100.70	

ACCOUNT Petty Cash — ACCOUNT NO. 1110

DATE 20--		ITEM	POST. REF.	DEBIT	CREDIT	BALANCE DEBIT	BALANCE CREDIT
Dec.	1	Balance	✔			200.00	

ACCOUNT Notes Receivable — ACCOUNT NO. 1115

DATE 20--		ITEM	POST. REF.	DEBIT	CREDIT	BALANCE DEBIT	BALANCE CREDIT
Dec.	1	Balance	✔			8,800.00	
	7		G12	3,600.00		12,400.00	
	26		CR12		5,800.00	6,600.00	
	30		G12		3,000.00	3,600.00	

ACCOUNT Interest Receivable — ACCOUNT NO. 1120

DATE 20--		ITEM	POST. REF.	DEBIT	CREDIT	BALANCE DEBIT	BALANCE CREDIT
Dec.	31		G13	24.00		24.00	
Jan.	1		G15		24.00	—	—

ACCOUNT Accounts Receivable — ACCOUNT NO. 1125

DATE 20--		ITEM	POST. REF.	DEBIT	CREDIT	BALANCE DEBIT	BALANCE CREDIT
Dec.	1	Balance	✔			9,553.00	
	7		G12		3,600.00	5,953.00	
	9		G12		2,460.00	3,493.00	
	18		G12	948.00		4,441.00	
	22		G12		127.20	4,313.80	
	30		G12	3,060.00		7,373.80	
	31		S12	5,248.80		12,622.60	
	31		CR12		4,728.00	7,894.60	

(Note: Dec. 31 postings from pp. 13-14 of the journal are part of the solution to Part B.)

Name ______________________ Date ______________ Class ______________

REINFORCEMENT ACTIVITY 3 PART A (continued)

ACCOUNT Allowance for Uncollectible Accounts — ACCOUNT NO. 1130

DATE		ITEM	POST. REF.	DEBIT	CREDIT	BALANCE DEBIT	BALANCE CREDIT
20-- Dec.	1	Balance	✔				42 60
	9		G12	2,460 00		2,417 40	
	18		G12		948 00	1,469 40	
	31		G13		3,600 00		2,130 60

ACCOUNT Merchandise Inventory — ACCOUNT NO. 1135

DATE		ITEM	POST. REF.	DEBIT	CREDIT	BALANCE DEBIT	BALANCE CREDIT
20-- Dec.	1	Balance	✔			74,176 95	
	31		G13	6,315 00		80,491 95	

ACCOUNT Supplies — ACCOUNT NO. 1140

DATE		ITEM	POST. REF.	DEBIT	CREDIT	BALANCE DEBIT	BALANCE CREDIT
20-- Dec.	1	Balance	✔			2,501 15	
	6		G12	362 40		2,863 55	
	10		CP23	223 00		3,086 55	
	31		CP23	12 50		3,099 05	
	31		G13		2,674 00	425 05	

ACCOUNT Prepaid Insurance — ACCOUNT NO. 1145

DATE		ITEM	POST. REF.	DEBIT	CREDIT	BALANCE DEBIT	BALANCE CREDIT
20-- Dec.	1	Balance	✔			8,600 00	
	31		G13		8,000 00	600 00	

ACCOUNT Office Equipment — ACCOUNT NO. 1205

DATE		ITEM	POST. REF.	DEBIT	CREDIT	BALANCE DEBIT	BALANCE CREDIT
20-- Dec.	1	Balance	✔			23,480 00	
	5		CP23	1,200 00		24,680 00	
	28		CR12		850 00	23,830 00	

REINFORCEMENT ACTIVITY 3 PART A (continued)

ACCOUNT Accumulated Depreciation—Office Equipment — ACCOUNT NO. 1210

DATE		ITEM	POST. REF.	DEBIT	CREDIT	BALANCE DEBIT	BALANCE CREDIT
20-- Dec.	1	Balance	✔				7,580.00
	28		G12		240.00		7,820.00
	28		CR12	660.00			7,160.00
	31		G13		6,520.00		13,680.00

ACCOUNT Warehouse Equipment — ACCOUNT NO. 1215

DATE		ITEM	POST. REF.	DEBIT	CREDIT	BALANCE DEBIT	BALANCE CREDIT
20-- Dec.	1	Balance	✔			29,010.00	
	14		CR12		2,900.00	26,110.00	

ACCOUNT Accumulated Depreciation—Warehouse Equipment — ACCOUNT NO. 1220

DATE		ITEM	POST. REF.	DEBIT	CREDIT	BALANCE DEBIT	BALANCE CREDIT
20-- Dec.	1	Balance	✔				8,480.00
	14		G12		440.00		8,920.00
	14		CR12	1,880.00			7,040.00
	31		G13		4,210.00		11,250.00

ACCOUNT Notes Payable — ACCOUNT NO. 2105

DATE		ITEM	POST. REF.	DEBIT	CREDIT	BALANCE DEBIT	BALANCE CREDIT
20-- Dec.	1	Balance	✔				20,000.00
	3		CP23	10,000.00			10,000.00
	28		CR12		6,000.00		16,000.00

ACCOUNT Interest Payable — ACCOUNT NO. 2110

DATE		ITEM	POST. REF.	DEBIT	CREDIT	BALANCE DEBIT	BALANCE CREDIT
20-- Dec.	31		G13		155.00		155.00
20-- Jan.	1		G15	155.00		—	—

Name ________________ Date ________ Class ________

REINFORCEMENT ACTIVITY 3 PART A (continued)

ACCOUNT Accounts Payable — ACCOUNT NO. 2115

DATE		ITEM	POST. REF.	DEBIT	CREDIT	BALANCE DEBIT	BALANCE CREDIT
20-- Dec.	1	Balance	✔				4087 25
	6		G12		362 40		4449 65
	14		G12	198 00			4251 65
	31		P12		22311 00		26562 65
	31		CP23	12450 00			14112 65

ACCOUNT Federal Income Tax Payable — ACCOUNT NO. 2120

DATE		ITEM	POST. REF.	DEBIT	CREDIT	BALANCE DEBIT	BALANCE CREDIT
20-- Dec.	31		G13		2103 16		2103 16
20-- Jan.	1		G15	2103 16		—	—

ACCOUNT Employee Income Tax Payable — ACCOUNT NO. 2125

DATE		ITEM	POST. REF.	DEBIT	CREDIT	BALANCE DEBIT	BALANCE CREDIT
20-- Dec.	1	Balance	✔				324 00
	15		CP23	324 00		—	—
	15		CP23		158 00		158 00
	31		CP23		152 00		310 00

ACCOUNT Social Security Tax Payable — ACCOUNT NO. 2130

DATE		ITEM	POST. REF.	DEBIT	CREDIT	BALANCE DEBIT	BALANCE CREDIT
20-- Dec.	1	Balance	✔				742 00
	15		G12		174 84		916 84
	15		CP23	742 00			174 84
	15		CP23		174 84		349 68
	31		G12		171 12		520 80
	31		CP23		171 12		691 92

REINFORCEMENT ACTIVITY 3 PART A (continued)

ACCOUNT Medicare Tax Payable ACCOUNT NO. 2135

DATE		ITEM	POST. REF.	DEBIT	CREDIT	BALANCE DEBIT	BALANCE CREDIT
20-- Dec.	1	Balance	✔				162 35
	15		G12		40 89		203 24
	15		CP23	162 35			40 89
	15		CP23		40 89		81 78
	31		G12		40 02		121 80
	31		CP23		40 02		161 82

ACCOUNT Sales Tax Payable ACCOUNT NO. 2140

DATE		ITEM	POST. REF.	DEBIT	CREDIT	BALANCE DEBIT	BALANCE CREDIT
20-- Dec.	1	Balance	✔				4942 68
	22		G12	7 20			4935 48
	31		S12		208 80		5144 28
	31		CR12		1066 38		6210 66

ACCOUNT Unemployment Tax Payable—Federal ACCOUNT NO. 2145

DATE		ITEM	POST. REF.	DEBIT	CREDIT	BALANCE DEBIT	BALANCE CREDIT
20-- Dec.	1	Balance	✔				13 05
	15		G12		4 48		17 53
	31		G12		4 00		21 53

ACCOUNT Unemployment Tax Payable—State ACCOUNT NO. 2150

DATE		ITEM	POST. REF.	DEBIT	CREDIT	BALANCE DEBIT	BALANCE CREDIT
20-- Dec.	1	Balance	✔				88 05
	15		G12		30 24		118 29
	31		G12		27 00		145 29

ACCOUNT Health Insurance Premiums Payable ACCOUNT NO. 2155

DATE		ITEM	POST. REF.	DEBIT	CREDIT	BALANCE DEBIT	BALANCE CREDIT
20-- Dec.	1	Balance	✔				725 00
	15		CP23		190 00		915 00
	31		CP23		190 00		1105 00

REINFORCEMENT ACTIVITY 3 PART A (continued)

ACCOUNT Dividends Payable — ACCOUNT NO. 2160

DATE		ITEM	POST. REF.	DEBIT	CREDIT	BALANCE DEBIT	BALANCE CREDIT
20-- Dec.	1	Balance	✔				5,000.00

ACCOUNT Capital Stock — ACCOUNT NO. 3105

DATE		ITEM	POST. REF.	DEBIT	CREDIT	BALANCE DEBIT	BALANCE CREDIT
20-- Dec.	1	Balance	✔				30,000.00

ACCOUNT Retained Earnings — ACCOUNT NO. 3110

DATE		ITEM	POST. REF.	DEBIT	CREDIT	BALANCE DEBIT	BALANCE CREDIT
20-- Dec.	1	Balance	✔				23,889.20
	31		G14		44,309.47		68,198.67
	31		G14	20,000.00			48,198.67

ACCOUNT Dividends — ACCOUNT NO. 3115

DATE		ITEM	POST. REF.	DEBIT	CREDIT	BALANCE DEBIT	BALANCE CREDIT
20-- Dec.	1	Balance	✔			20,000.00	
	31		G14		20,000.00	—	—

ACCOUNT Income Summary — ACCOUNT NO. 3120

DATE		ITEM	POST. REF.	DEBIT	CREDIT	BALANCE DEBIT	BALANCE CREDIT
20-- Dec.	31		G13		6,315.00		6,315.00
	31		G14		787,225.98		793,540.98
	31		G14	749,231.51			44,309.47
	31		G14	44,309.47		—	—

ACCOUNT Sales — ACCOUNT NO. 4105

DATE		ITEM	POST. REF.	DEBIT	CREDIT	BALANCE DEBIT	BALANCE CREDIT
20-- Dec.	1	Balance	✔				756,397.90
	31		S12		5,040.00		761,437.90
	31		CR12		17,773.00		779,210.90
	31		G14	779,210.90		—	—

REINFORCEMENT ACTIVITY 3 PART A (continued)

ACCOUNT Sales Discount — ACCOUNT NO. 4110

DATE		ITEM	POST. REF.	DEBIT	CREDIT	BALANCE DEBIT	BALANCE CREDIT
20-- Dec.	1	Balance	✔			1,878.60	
	31		CR12	10.60		1,889.20	
	31		G14		1,889.20	—	—

ACCOUNT Sales Returns and Allowances — ACCOUNT NO. 4115

DATE		ITEM	POST. REF.	DEBIT	CREDIT	BALANCE DEBIT	BALANCE CREDIT
20-- Dec.	1	Balance	✔			6,054.80	
	22		G12	120.00		6,174.80	
	31		G14		6,174.80	—	—

ACCOUNT Purchases — ACCOUNT NO. 5105

DATE		ITEM	POST. REF.	DEBIT	CREDIT	BALANCE DEBIT	BALANCE CREDIT
20-- Dec.	1	Balance	✔			506,354.40	
	21		CP23	357.00		506,711.40	
	31		P12	22,311.00		529,022.40	
	31		G14		529,022.40	—	—

ACCOUNT Purchases Discount — ACCOUNT NO. 5110

DATE		ITEM	POST. REF.	DEBIT	CREDIT	BALANCE DEBIT	BALANCE CREDIT
20-- Dec.	1	Balance	✔				3,493.32
	31		CP23		102.76		3,596.08
	31		G14	3,596.08		—	—

ACCOUNT Purchases Returns and Allowances — ACCOUNT NO. 5115

DATE		ITEM	POST. REF.	DEBIT	CREDIT	BALANCE DEBIT	BALANCE CREDIT
20-- Dec.	1	Balance	✔				3,038.00
	14		G12		198.00		3,236.00
	31		G14	3,236.00		—	—

Name ______________________ Date ____________ Class ____________

REINFORCEMENT ACTIVITY 3 PART A (continued)

ACCOUNT Advertising Expense — ACCOUNT NO. 6105

DATE		ITEM	POST. REF.	DEBIT	CREDIT	BALANCE DEBIT	BALANCE CREDIT
20-- Dec.	1	Balance	✔			9,556.70	
	31		CP23	50.00		9,606.70	
	31		G14		9,606.70	—	—

ACCOUNT Cash Short and Over — ACCOUNT NO. 6110

DATE		ITEM	POST. REF.	DEBIT	CREDIT	BALANCE DEBIT	BALANCE CREDIT
20-- Dec.	1	Balance	✔			20.00	
	31		CP23	0.09		20.09	
	31		G14		20.09	—	—

ACCOUNT Credit Card Fee Expense — ACCOUNT NO. 6115

DATE		ITEM	POST. REF.	DEBIT	CREDIT	BALANCE DEBIT	BALANCE CREDIT
20-- Dec.	1	Balance	✔			14,111.40	
	30		CP23	418.00		14,529.40	
	31		G14		14,529.40	—	—

ACCOUNT Depreciation Expense—Office Equipment — ACCOUNT NO. 6120

DATE		ITEM	POST. REF.	DEBIT	CREDIT	BALANCE DEBIT	BALANCE CREDIT
20-- Dec.	28		G12	240.00		240.00	
	31		G13	6,520.00		6,760.00	
	31		G14		6,760.00	—	—

ACCOUNT Depreciation Expense—Warehouse Equipment — ACCOUNT NO. 6125

DATE		ITEM	POST. REF.	DEBIT	CREDIT	BALANCE DEBIT	BALANCE CREDIT
20-- Dec.	14		G12	440.00		440.00	
	31		G13	4,210.00		4,650.00	
	31		G14		4,650.00	—	—

REINFORCEMENT ACTIVITY 3 PART A (continued)

ACCOUNT Insurance Expense ACCOUNT NO. 6130

DATE		ITEM	POST. REF.	DEBIT	CREDIT	BALANCE DEBIT	BALANCE CREDIT
20-- Dec.	31		G13	8,000.00		8,000.00	
	31		G14		8,000.00	—	—

ACCOUNT Miscellaneous Expense ACCOUNT NO. 6135

DATE		ITEM	POST. REF.	DEBIT	CREDIT	BALANCE DEBIT	BALANCE CREDIT
20-- Dec.	1	Balance	✔			5,733.95	
	19		CP23	72.00		5,805.95	
	31		CP23	22.37		5,828.32	
	31		G14		5,828.32	—	—

ACCOUNT Payroll Taxes Expense ACCOUNT NO. 6140

DATE		ITEM	POST. REF.	DEBIT	CREDIT	BALANCE DEBIT	BALANCE CREDIT
20-- Dec.	1	Balance	✔			10,176.85	
	15		G12	250.45		10,427.30	
	31		G12	242.14		10,669.44	
	31		G14		10,669.44	—	—

ACCOUNT Rent Expense ACCOUNT NO. 6145

DATE		ITEM	POST. REF.	DEBIT	CREDIT	BALANCE DEBIT	BALANCE CREDIT
20-- Dec.	1	Balance	✔			19,250.00	
	1		CP23	1,750.00		21,000.00	
	31		G14		21,000.00	—	—

ACCOUNT Repairs Expense ACCOUNT NO. 6150

DATE		ITEM	POST. REF.	DEBIT	CREDIT	BALANCE DEBIT	BALANCE CREDIT
20-- Dec.		Balance	✔			1,394.80	
	31		G14		1,394.80	—	—

Name ______________________ Date ______________ Class ______________

REINFORCEMENT ACTIVITY 3 PART A (continued)

ACCOUNT Salary Expense — ACCOUNT NO. 6155

DATE		ITEM	POST. REF.	DEBIT	CREDIT	BALANCE DEBIT	BALANCE CREDIT
20-- Dec.	1	Balance	✔			99 298 00	
	15		CP23	2 820 00		102 118 00	
	31		CP23	2 760 00		104 878 00	
	31		G14		104 878 00	—	—

ACCOUNT Supplies Expense — ACCOUNT NO. 6160

DATE		ITEM	POST. REF.	DEBIT	CREDIT	BALANCE DEBIT	BALANCE CREDIT
20-- Dec.	31		G13	2 674 00		2 674 00	
	31		G14		2 674 00	—	—

ACCOUNT Uncollectible Accounts Expense — ACCOUNT NO. 6165

DATE		ITEM	POST. REF.	DEBIT	CREDIT	BALANCE DEBIT	BALANCE CREDIT
20-- Dec.	31		G13	3 600 00		3 600 00	
	31		G14		3 600 00	—	—

ACCOUNT Utilities Expense — ACCOUNT NO. 6170

DATE		ITEM	POST. REF.	DEBIT	CREDIT	BALANCE DEBIT	BALANCE CREDIT
20-- Dec.	1	Balance	✔			6 890 00	
	17		CP23	346 20		7 236 20	
	31		G14		7 236 20	—	—

ACCOUNT Gain on Plant Assets — ACCOUNT NO. 7105

DATE		ITEM	POST. REF.	DEBIT	CREDIT	BALANCE DEBIT	BALANCE CREDIT
20-- Dec.	1	Balance	✔				365 00
	14		CR12		380 00		745 00
	31		G14	745 00		—	—

REINFORCEMENT ACTIVITY 3 PART A (concluded)

ACCOUNT Interest Income ACCOUNT NO. 7110

DATE		ITEM	POST. REF.	DEBIT	CREDIT	BALANCE DEBIT	BALANCE CREDIT
20-- Dec.	1	Balance	✔				180 00
	26		CR12		174 00		354 00
	30		G12		60 00		414 00
	31		G13		24 00		438 00
	31		G14	438 00		—	—
20-- Jan.	1		G15	24 00		24 00	

ACCOUNT Interest Expense ACCOUNT NO. 8105

DATE		ITEM	POST. REF.	DEBIT	CREDIT	BALANCE DEBIT	BALANCE CREDIT
20-- Dec.	1	Balance	✔			2300 00	
	3		CP23	450 00		2750 00	
	31		G13	155 00		2905 00	
	31		G14		2905 00	—	—
20-- Jan.	1		G15		155 00		155 00

ACCOUNT Loss on Plant Assets ACCOUNT NO. 8110

DATE		ITEM	POST. REF.	DEBIT	CREDIT	BALANCE DEBIT	BALANCE CREDIT
20-- Dec.	1	Balance	✔			250 00	
	28		CR12	40 00		290 00	
	31		G14		290 00	—	—

ACCOUNT Federal Income Tax Expense ACCOUNT NO. 9105

DATE		ITEM	POST. REF.	DEBIT	CREDIT	BALANCE DEBIT	BALANCE CREDIT
20-- Dec.	1	Balance	✔			6000 00	
	31		G13	2103 16		8103 16	
	31		G14		8103 16	—	—
20-- Jan.	1		G15		2103 16		2103 16

Study Guide 21

Name	Perfect Score	Your Score
Identifying Accounting Concepts and Practices	15 Pts.	
Analyzing Accounts Affected by Accrued Revenue and Accrued Expenses	18 Pts.	
Analyzing Accrued Revenue and Accrued Expenses	11 Pts.	
Total	44 Pts.	

Part One—Identifying Accounting Concepts and Practices

Directions: For each of the following items, select the choice that best completes the statement. Print the letter identifying your choice in the Answers column.

	Answers
1. At the end of a fiscal period, each expense that has been incurred but not paid should be recorded as (A) an adjusting entry (B) a reversing entry (C) a closing entry (D) an opening entry. (p. 616)	1. *A*
2. Revenue earned in one fiscal period but not received until a later fiscal period is called (A) accrued expense (B) accrued interest expense (C) accrued revenue (D) deferred interest income. (p. 616)	2. *C*
3. Recording adjusting entries for the fiscal period in which the revenue has been earned regardless of when it will be received is an application of the accounting concept (A) Objective Evidence (B) Realization of Revenue (C) Adequate Disclosure (D) Historical Cost. (p. 616)	3. *B*
4. At the end of a fiscal period, any revenue that has been earned but not received should be credited to an appropriate (A) revenue account (B) expense account (C) liability account (D) asset account. (p. 616)	4. *A*
5. Interest earned but not yet received is called (A) accrued interest income (B) deferred interest income (C) deferred earned income (D) none of these. (p. 617)	5. *A*
6. Interest Receivable is (A) an asset (B) a liability (C) revenue (D) an expense. (p. 618)	6. *A*
7. An entry made at the beginning of one fiscal period to reverse an adjusting entry made in the previous fiscal period is called (A) a debit entry (B) a credit entry (C) a reversing entry (D) none of these. (p. 619)	7. *C*
8. A reversing entry for accrued interest income results in a debit to (A) Interest Receivable (B) Notes Receivable (C) Income Summary (D) Interest Income. (p. 619)	8. *D*
9. A reversing entry for accrued interest income will result in an account balance of (A) Interest Receivable debit (B) Interest Income debit (C) Interest Receivable credit (D) Interest Income credit. (p. 619)	9. *B*
10. Expenses incurred in one fiscal period but not paid until a later fiscal period are called (A) accrued interest expenses (B) accrued expenses (C) accrued income expenses (D) accrued interest receivable. (p. 622)	10. *B*
11. At the end of a fiscal period, each expense that has been incurred but not paid should be debited to an appropriate (A) revenue account (B) expense account (C) asset account (D) liability account. (p. 622)	11. *B*
12. Interest incurred but not yet paid is called (A) accrued income expense (B) earned income (C) accrued interest expense (D) deferred interest expense. (p. 622)	12. *C*
13. At the end of a fiscal period, each expense that has been incurred but not paid should be credited to an appropriate (A) revenue account (B) expense account (C) asset account (D) liability account. (p. 622)	13. *D*
14. A reversing entry for accrued interest expense will result in an account balance of (A) Interest Payable debit (B) Interest Payable credit (C) Interest Expense debit (D) Interest Expense credit. (p. 624)	14. *D*
15. An adjusting entry normally is reversed if the adjusting entry creates a balance in (A) a revenue or expense account (B) a revenue and liability account (C) an expense and asset account (D) an asset or liability account. (p. 626)	15. *D*

Part Two—Analyzing Accounts Affected by Accrued Revenue and Accrued Expenses

Directions: Analyze each of the following entries into debit and credit parts. Print the letter identifying your choice in the proper Answers columns. Determine in which journal each of the transactions are to be recorded.

G—General journal CP—Cash payments journal CR—Cash receipts journal

Account Titles	Transactions	Answers Journal	Answers Debit	Answers Credit
A. Cash	**1–2–3.** Recorded an adjustment for accrued interest income. (p. 617)	1. *G*	2. *E*	3. *C*
B. Interest Expense	**4–5–6.** Reversed an adjusting entry for accrued interest income. (p. 619)	4. *G*	5. *C*	6. *E*
C. Interest Income	**7–8–9.** Received cash for the maturity value of a 90-day, 12% note. (p. 620)	7. *CR*	8. *A*	9. *G, C*
D. Interest Payable	**10–11–12.** Recorded an adjustment for accrued interest expense. (p. 622)	10. *G*	11. *B*	12. *D*
E. Interest Receivable	**13–14–15.** Reversed an adjusting entry for accrued interest expense. (p. 624)	13. *G*	14. *D*	15. *B*
F. Notes Payable	**16–17–18.** Paid cash for the maturity value of a note payable plus interest. (p. 625)	16. *CP*	17. *F, B*	18. *A*
G. Notes Receivable				

Name ______________________ Date __________ Class __________

Part Three—Analyzing Accrued Revenue and Accrued Expenses

Directions: Place a *T* for True or an *F* for False in the Answers column to show whether each of the following statements is true or false.

		Answers
1.	Revenue should be recorded when the revenue is earned. (p. 616)	**1.** *T*
2.	Adjusting entries are made at the beginning of each fiscal period. (p. 616)	**2.** *F*
3.	The adjustment for accrued interest income is planned on a work sheet. (p. 617)	**3.** *T*
4.	Accrued interest income is credited to the interest income account. (p. 617)	**4.** *T*
5.	When an adjusting entry for accrued interest income is made, Interest Receivable is debited. (p. 617)	**5.** *T*
6.	Accrued interest is calculated by multiplying principal times interest rate times time as a fraction of a year. (p. 617)	**6.** *T*
7.	Reversing entries are made on the last day of the fiscal period. (p. 619)	**7.** *F*
8.	A reversing entry for interest income reduces the balance of Interest Receivable. (p. 619)	**8.** *T*
9.	At the end of a fiscal period, the Interest Expense balance after adjustments shows the amount of interest expense that has been incurred in that fiscal period. (p. 622)	**9.** *T*
10.	An Interest Payable credit balance is accrued interest expense incurred in the current year but to be paid in the next year. (p. 622)	**10.** *T*
11.	When a reversing entry is made for accrued interest expense, a debit entry is required to Interest Payable. (p. 624)	**11.** *T*

Study Skills

Following Directions

"I thought you said the paper was due next week."
"Isn't this what I was supposed to do?"
"When did you tell us to do that?"

These are remarks often heard at school. A student has missed a deadline; another has done the wrong assignment; a third did not recall receiving the assignment at all. All three will receive a poor grade when they could easily have made a good grade. Why? The reason is that they did not listen to directions or they did not follow directions.

Listen Attentively

In order to meet all deadlines, you must listen very carefully when an assignment is made. Your teacher will probably give complete directions, including due date. If any part of the assignment is not clear, you should ask for a clarification when the assignment is made. If you have any doubt about the format, the content, or the due date, you should ask immediately. Do not wait to ask until it is time to turn in the assignment. You may miss the deadline altogether, or you may not allow yourself enough time to complete the assignment properly.

Follow Directions to the Letter

You must complete each assignment according to the directions your teacher gives. For example, you may be asked to write a major paper. Your teacher will probably give you detailed instructions on how information is to be collected and how it is to be presented in the paper.

If your teacher asks you to obtain references from at least three books, be sure that you do. Four books will be satisfactory, but two will not. If asked to use current references, articles three or four years old will not be satisfactory. If your teacher asks you to use charts and graphs to illustrate your points, be sure that you include them.

Use the Right Format

There are many formats that are acceptable for preparing most assignments. If your teacher asks you to use a specific format, you must follow it, even if you prefer another. If no format is specified for a writing assignment, you should ask. If there is no preference, you should use a simple format and be completely consistent.

Right on Schedule

If you have a major assignment given to you at the beginning of the term, begin work early, following all directions. If you leave all the work to do at the last minute, the quality will suffer and so will your grade. It is not usually possible to collect a large amount of information overnight. In addition, if you try to do all your work just before it is due, you will have no time to reflect on the work and change any part that you do not like.

Be absolutely sure to turn your assignment in right on schedule. It should not be necessary for you to ask for extra time to finish it.

Improve Your Grades

Following directions to the letter is very easy; however, some students never seem to realize this. One of the easiest ways to improve your grades is to prepare every assignment exactly as it is assigned. The result will show in your grades.

Name ______________________ Date ______________ Class ______________

21-1 WORK TOGETHER, p. 621

Journalizing and posting entries for accrued revenue

1.

Marris Corporation
Work Sheet
For Year Ended December 31, 20 – –

	ACCOUNT TITLE	1 TRIAL BALANCE DEBIT	2 TRIAL BALANCE CREDIT	3 ADJUSTMENTS DEBIT	4 ADJUSTMENTS CREDIT
4	Interest Receivable			(a) 60 00	
50	Interest Income		1 545 00		(a) 60 00

2., 3.

GENERAL JOURNAL — PAGE 14

	DATE		ACCOUNT TITLE	DOC. NO.	POST. REF.	DEBIT	CREDIT	
1			*Adjusting Entries*					1
2	20 – – Dec.	31	*Interest Receivable*		1120	60 00		2
3			*Interest Income*		7110		60 00	3
4								4
5			*Closing Entries*					5
6	20 – – Dec.	31	*Interest Income*		7110	1 605 00		6
7			*Income Summary*		3120		1 605 00	7
8								8

4.

GENERAL JOURNAL — PAGE 15

	DATE		ACCOUNT TITLE	DOC. NO.	POST. REF.	DEBIT	CREDIT	
1			*Reversing Entries*					1
2	20 – – Jan.	1	*Interest Income*		7110	60 00		2
3			*Interest Receivable*		1120		60 00	3
4								4

5.

CASH RECEIPTS JOURNAL

PAGE 16

	DATE		ACCOUNT TITLE	DOC. NO.	POST. REF.	1 GENERAL DEBIT	2 GENERAL CREDIT	3 ACCOUNTS RECEIVABLE CREDIT	4 SALES CREDIT	5 SALES TAX PAYABLE CREDIT	6 SALES DISCOUNT DEBIT	7 CASH DEBIT	
1	20-- Mar.	16	Notes Receivable	R32	1115		4 000 00					4 160 00	1
2			Interest Income		7110		160 00						2
3													3
4													4
5													5
6													6
7													7
8													8
9													9
10													10
11													11
12													12
13													13
14													14
15													15
16													16
17													17
18													18
19													19
20													20
21													21
22													22
23													23
24													24

Name ______________________ Date ______________ Class ______________

21-1 WORK TOGETHER (concluded)

2., 3., 4., 5.

GENERAL LEDGER

ACCOUNT Notes Receivable — ACCOUNT NO. 1115

DATE		ITEM	POST. REF.	DEBIT	CREDIT	BALANCE DEBIT	BALANCE CREDIT
Nov.	16		G11	4,000.00		4,000.00	
20-- Mar.	16		CR16		4,000.00	—	—

ACCOUNT Interest Receivable — ACCOUNT NO. 1120

DATE		ITEM	POST. REF.	DEBIT	CREDIT	BALANCE DEBIT	BALANCE CREDIT
20-- Dec.	31		G14	60.00		60.00	
20-- Jan.	1		G15		60.00	—	—

ACCOUNT Income Summary — ACCOUNT NO. 3120

DATE		ITEM	POST. REF.	DEBIT	CREDIT	BALANCE DEBIT	BALANCE CREDIT
20-- Dec.	31		G14		160.50		160.50

ACCOUNT Interest Income — ACCOUNT NO. 7110

DATE		ITEM	POST. REF.	DEBIT	CREDIT	BALANCE DEBIT	BALANCE CREDIT
Dec.	31		CR15		15.00		154.50
	31		G14		6.00		160.50
	31		G14	160.50		—	—
20-- Jan.	1		G15	60.00		60.00	
Mar.	16		CR16		160.00		100.00

21-1 ON YOUR OWN, p. 621

Journalizing and posting entries for accrued revenue

1.

ExMark, Inc.
Work Sheet
For Year Ended December 31, 20 – –

	ACCOUNT TITLE	TRIAL BALANCE DEBIT (1)	TRIAL BALANCE CREDIT (2)	ADJUSTMENTS DEBIT (3)	ADJUSTMENTS CREDIT (4)
4	Interest Receivable			(a) 50 00	
50	Interest Income		692 00		(a) 50 00

2., 3.

GENERAL JOURNAL PAGE 14

	DATE		ACCOUNT TITLE	DOC. NO.	POST. REF.	DEBIT	CREDIT	
1			*Adjusting Entries*					1
2	20-- Dec.	31	*Interest Receivable*		1120	50 00		2
3			*Interest Income*		7110		50 00	3
4								4
5			*Closing Entries*					5
6	20-- Dec.	31	*Interest Income*		7110	742 00		6
7			*Income Summary*		3120		742 00	7
8								8

4.

GENERAL JOURNAL PAGE 15

	DATE		ACCOUNT TITLE	DOC. NO.	POST. REF.	DEBIT	CREDIT	
1			*Reversing Entries*					1
2	20-- Jan.	1	*Interest Income*		7110	50 00		2
3			*Interest Receivable*		1120		50 00	3
4								4

21-1 ON YOUR OWN (continued)

5.

CASH RECEIPTS JOURNAL PAGE 19

	DATE	ACCOUNT TITLE	DOC. NO.	POST. REF.	1 GENERAL DEBIT	2 GENERAL CREDIT	3 ACCOUNTS RECEIVABLE CREDIT	4 SALES CREDIT	5 SALES TAX PAYABLE CREDIT	6 SALES DISCOUNT DEBIT	7 CASH DEBIT	
1	20-- Mar. 1	Notes Receivable	R65	1115		6 000 00					6 150 00	1
2		Interest Income		7110		150 00						2
3												3
4												4
5												5
6												6
7												7
8												8
9												9
10												10
11												11
12												12
13												13
14												14
15												15
16												16
17												17
18												18
19												19
20												20
21												21
22												22
23												23
24												24

21-1 ON YOUR OWN (concluded)

2., 3., 4., 5.

GENERAL LEDGER

ACCOUNT Notes Receivable — ACCOUNT NO. 1115

DATE		ITEM	POST. REF.	DEBIT	CREDIT	BALANCE DEBIT	BALANCE CREDIT
Dec.	1		G11	6 000 00		6 000 00	
20-- Mar.	1		CR19		6 000 00	—	—

ACCOUNT Interest Receivable — ACCOUNT NO. 1120

DATE		ITEM	POST. REF.	DEBIT	CREDIT	BALANCE DEBIT	BALANCE CREDIT
20-- Dec.	31		G14	50 00		50 00	
20-- Jan.	1		G15		50 00	—	—

ACCOUNT Income Summary — ACCOUNT NO. 3120

DATE		ITEM	POST. REF.	DEBIT	CREDIT	BALANCE DEBIT	BALANCE CREDIT
20-- Dec.	31		G14		742 00		742 00

ACCOUNT Interest Income — ACCOUNT NO. 7110

DATE		ITEM	POST. REF.	DEBIT	CREDIT	BALANCE DEBIT	BALANCE CREDIT
Dec.	31		CR15		87 50		692 00
	31		G14		50 00		742 00
	31		G14	742 00		—	—
20-- Jan.	1		G15	50 00		50 00	
Mar.	1		CR19		150 00		100 00

Name ______________________ Date ____________ Class ____________

21-2 WORK TOGETHER, p. 627

Journalizing and posting entries for accrued expenses

1.

Powers Corporation

Work Sheet

For Year Ended December 31, 20 – –

	ACCOUNT TITLE	1 TRIAL BALANCE DEBIT	2 TRIAL BALANCE CREDIT	3 ADJUSTMENTS DEBIT	4 ADJUSTMENTS CREDIT
15	Interest Payable				(h) 20 00
51	Interest Expense	8 477 00		(h) 20 00	

2., 3.

GENERAL JOURNAL PAGE 14

	DATE		ACCOUNT TITLE	DOC. NO.	POST. REF.	DEBIT	CREDIT	
1			*Adjusting Entries*					1
2	20 – – *Dec.*	*31*	*Interest Expense*		*8105*	*20 00*		2
3			*Interest Payable*		*2110*		*20 00*	3
4								4
5			*Closing Entries*					5
6	20 – – *Dec.*	*31*	*Income Summary*		*3120*	*8 497 00*		6
7			*Interest Expense*		*8105*		*8 497 00*	7
8								8

4.

GENERAL JOURNAL PAGE 15

	DATE		ACCOUNT TITLE	DOC. NO.	POST. REF.	DEBIT	CREDIT	
1			*Reversing Entries*					1
2	20 – – *Jan.*	*1*	*Interest Payable*		*2110*	*20 00*		2
3			*Interest Expense*		*8105*		*20 00*	3
4								4

5.

CASH PAYMENTS JOURNAL

PAGE 25

	DATE		ACCOUNT TITLE	CK. NO.	POST. REF.	1 GENERAL DEBIT	2 GENERAL CREDIT	3 ACCOUNTS PAYABLE DEBIT	4 PURCHASES DISCOUNT CREDIT	5 CASH CREDIT	
1	20-- Mar.	1	Notes Payable	543	2105	2000 00				2060 00	1
2			Interest Expense		8105	60 00					2
3											3
4											4
5											5
6											6
7											7
8											8
9											9
10											10
11											11
12											12
13											13
14											14
15											15
16											16
17											17
18											18
19											19
20											20
21											21
22											22
23											23
24											24

Name ______ Date ______ Class ______

21-2 WORK TOGETHER (concluded)

2., 3., 4., 5. **GENERAL LEDGER**

ACCOUNT Notes Payable — ACCOUNT NO. 2105

DATE		ITEM	POST. REF.	DEBIT	CREDIT	BALANCE DEBIT	BALANCE CREDIT
Dec.	1		CR13		2,000.00		2,000.00
20-- Mar.	1		CP25	2,000.00		—	—

ACCOUNT Interest Payable — ACCOUNT NO. 2110

DATE		ITEM	POST. REF.	DEBIT	CREDIT	BALANCE DEBIT	BALANCE CREDIT
20-- Dec.	31		G14		20.00		20.00
20-- Jan.	1		G15	20.00		—	—

ACCOUNT Income Summary — ACCOUNT NO. 3120

DATE		ITEM	POST. REF.	DEBIT	CREDIT	BALANCE DEBIT	BALANCE CREDIT
20-- Dec.	31		G14	8,497.00		8,497.00	

ACCOUNT Interest Expense — ACCOUNT NO. 8105

DATE		ITEM	POST. REF.	DEBIT	CREDIT	BALANCE DEBIT	BALANCE CREDIT
Dec.	31		CP19	160.00		8,477.00	
	31		G14	20.00		8,497.00	
	31		G14		8,497.00	—	—
20-- Jan.	1		G15		20.00		20.00
Mar.	1		CP25	60.00		40.00	

21-2 ON YOUR OWN, p. 627

Journalizing and posting entries for accrued expenses

1.

Latham Industries
Work Sheet
For Year Ended December 31, 20 – –

	Account Title	Trial Balance Debit (1)	Trial Balance Credit (2)	Adjustments Debit (3)	Adjustments Credit (4)
15	Interest Payable				(h) 93 75
51	Interest Expense	4,708 25		(h) 93 75	

2., 3.

GENERAL JOURNAL — PAGE 14

	Date		Account Title	Doc. No.	Post. Ref.	Debit	Credit	
1			*Adjusting Entries*					1
2	20– – Dec.	31	Interest Expense		8105	93 75		2
3			Interest Payable		2110		93 75	3
4								4
5			*Closing Entries*					5
6	20– – Dec.	31	Income Summary		3120	4,802 00		6
7			Interest Expense		8105		4,802 00	7
8								8

4.

GENERAL JOURNAL — PAGE 15

	Date		Account Title	Doc. No.	Post. Ref.	Debit	Credit	
1			*Reversing Entries*					1
2	20– – Jan.	1	Interest Payable		2110	93 75		2
3			Interest Expense		8105		93 75	3
4								4

Name ______________________ Date ______________ Class ______________

21-2 ON YOUR OWN (continued)

5.

CASH PAYMENTS JOURNAL

PAGE 30

					1	2	3	4	5	
	DATE	ACCOUNT TITLE	CK. NO.	POST. REF.	GENERAL DEBIT	GENERAL CREDIT	ACCOUNTS PAYABLE DEBIT	PURCHASES DISCOUNT CREDIT	CASH CREDIT	
1	20-- Apr. 15	Notes Payable	668	2105	5 000 00				5 225 00	1
2		Interest Expense		8105	225 00					2
3										3
4										4
5										5
6										6
7										7
8										8
9										9
10										10
11										11
12										12
13										13
14										14
15										15
16										16
17										17
18										18
19										19
20										20
21										21
22										22
23										23
24										24

21-2 ON YOUR OWN (concluded)

2., 3., 4., 5. **GENERAL LEDGER**

ACCOUNT Notes Payable ACCOUNT NO. 2105

DATE		ITEM	POST. REF.	DEBIT	CREDIT	BALANCE DEBIT	BALANCE CREDIT
Oct.	17		CR9		5000 00		5000 00
20-- Apr.	15		CP30	5000 00		—	—

ACCOUNT Interest Payable ACCOUNT NO. 2110

DATE		ITEM	POST. REF.	DEBIT	CREDIT	BALANCE DEBIT	BALANCE CREDIT
20-- Dec.	31		G14		93 75		93 75
20-- Jan.	1		G15	93 75		—	—

ACCOUNT Income Summary ACCOUNT NO. 3120

DATE		ITEM	POST. REF.	DEBIT	CREDIT	BALANCE DEBIT	BALANCE CREDIT
20-- Dec.	31		G14	4802 00		4802 00	

ACCOUNT Interest Expense ACCOUNT NO. 8105

DATE		ITEM	POST. REF.	DEBIT	CREDIT	BALANCE DEBIT	BALANCE CREDIT
Dec.	31		CP24	50 00		4708 25	
	31		G14	93 75		4802 00	
	31		G14		4802 00	—	—
20-- Jan.	1		G15		93 75		93 75
Apr.	15		CP30	225 00		131 25	

Name ____________________ Date ____________ Class ____________

21-1 APPLICATION PROBLEM, p. 629

Journalizing and posting entries for accrued revenue

1.

Velma Parts Company
Work Sheet
For Year Ended December 31, 20 – –

	Account Title	1 Trial Balance Debit	2 Trial Balance Credit	3 Adjustments Debit	4 Adjustments Credit
4	Interest Receivable			(a) 123.75	
50	Interest Income		1,967.50		(a) 123.75

2., 3.

GENERAL JOURNAL — PAGE 14

	Date		Account Title	Doc. No.	Post. Ref.	Debit	Credit	
1			*Adjusting Entries*					1
2	20-- Dec.	31	Interest Receivable		1120	123.75		2
3			Interest Income		7110		123.75	3
4								4
5			*Closing Entries*					5
6	20-- Dec.	31	Interest Income		7110	2,091.25		6
7			Income Summary		3120		2,091.25	7
8								8

4.

GENERAL JOURNAL — PAGE 15

	Date		Account Title	Doc. No.	Post. Ref.	Debit	Credit	
1			*Reversing Entries*					1
2	20-- Jan.	1	Interest Income		7110	123.75		2
3			Interest Receivable		1120		123.75	3
4								4

21-1 APPLICATION PROBLEM (continued)

5.

CASH RECEIPTS JOURNAL

PAGE 8

	DATE		ACCOUNT TITLE	DOC. NO.	POST. REF.	1 GENERAL DEBIT	2 GENERAL CREDIT	3 ACCOUNTS RECEIVABLE CREDIT	4 SALES CREDIT	5 SALES TAX PAYABLE CREDIT	6 SALES DISCOUNT DEBIT	7 CASH DEBIT	
1	20-- Mar.	6	*Notes Receivable*	R457	1115		8 100 00					8 370 00	1
2			*Interest Income*		7110		270 00						2
3													3
4													4
5													5
6													6
7													7
8													8
9													9
10													10
11													11
12													12
13													13
14													14
15													15
16													16
17													17
18													18
19													19
20													20
21													21
22													22
23													23
24													24

Name ______________________ Date ______________ Class ______________

21-1 APPLICATION PROBLEM (concluded)

2., 3., 4., 5. **GENERAL LEDGER**

ACCOUNT Notes Receivable ACCOUNT NO. 1115

DATE		ITEM	POST. REF.	DEBIT	CREDIT	BALANCE DEBIT	BALANCE CREDIT
Nov.	6		G11	8,100.00		8,100.00	
20-- Mar.	6		CR8		8,100.00	—	—

ACCOUNT Interest Receivable ACCOUNT NO. 1120

DATE		ITEM	POST. REF.	DEBIT	CREDIT	BALANCE DEBIT	BALANCE CREDIT
20-- Dec.	31		G14	123.75		123.75	
20-- Jan.	1		G15		123.75	—	—

ACCOUNT Income Summary ACCOUNT NO. 3120

DATE		ITEM	POST. REF.	DEBIT	CREDIT	BALANCE DEBIT	BALANCE CREDIT
20-- Dec.	31		G14		2,091.25		2,091.25

ACCOUNT Interest Income ACCOUNT NO. 7110

DATE		ITEM	POST. REF.	DEBIT	CREDIT	BALANCE DEBIT	BALANCE CREDIT
Dec.	31		CR18		25.00		1,967.50
Dec.	31		G14		123.75		2,091.25
	31		G14	2,091.25		—	—
20-- Jan.	1		G15	123.75		123.75	
Mar.	6		CR8		270.00		146.25

21-2 APPLICATION PROBLEM, p. 629

Journalizing and posting entries for accrued expenses

1.

Delmar Plumbing Supply
Work Sheet
For Year Ended December 31, 20 – –

	ACCOUNT TITLE	1 TRIAL BALANCE DEBIT	2 TRIAL BALANCE CREDIT	3 ADJUSTMENTS DEBIT	4 ADJUSTMENTS CREDIT
15	Interest Payable				(h) 100.00
51	Interest Expense	8,489.00		(h) 100.00	

2., 3.

GENERAL JOURNAL PAGE 14

	DATE		ACCOUNT TITLE	DOC. NO.	POST. REF.	DEBIT	CREDIT	
1			*Adjusting Entries*					1
2	20-- Dec.	31	Interest Expense		8105	100.00		2
3			Interest Payable		2110		100.00	3
4								4
5			*Closing Entries*					5
6	20-- Dec.	31	Income Summary		3120	8,589.00		6
7			Interest Expense		8105		8,589.00	7
8								8

4.

GENERAL JOURNAL PAGE 15

	DATE		ACCOUNT TITLE	DOC. NO.	POST. REF.	DEBIT	CREDIT	
1			*Reversing Entries*					1
2	20-- Jan.	1	Interest Payable		2110	100.00		2
3			Interest Expense		8105		100.00	3
4								4

Name ______________________ Date ______________ Class ______________

21-2 APPLICATION PROBLEM (continued)

5.

CASH PAYMENTS JOURNAL

PAGE 27

	DATE		ACCOUNT TITLE	CK. NO.	POST. REF.	1 GENERAL DEBIT	2 GENERAL CREDIT	3 ACCOUNTS PAYABLE DEBIT	4 PURCHASES DISCOUNT CREDIT	5 CASH CREDIT	
1	20-- May	30	Notes Payable	756	2105	12 000 00				12 600 00	1
2			Interest Expense		8105	600 00					2
3											3
4											4
5											5
6											6
7											7
8											8
9											9
10											10
11											11
12											12
13											13
14											14
15											15
16											16
17											17
18											18
19											19
20											20
21											21
22											22
23											23
24											24

2., 3., 4., 5. **GENERAL LEDGER**

ACCOUNT Notes Payable ACCOUNT NO. 2105

DATE		ITEM	POST. REF.	DEBIT	CREDIT	BALANCE DEBIT	BALANCE CREDIT
Dec.	1		CR12		12,000.00		12,000.00
20-- May	30		CP27	12,000.00		—	—

ACCOUNT Interest Payable ACCOUNT NO. 2110

DATE		ITEM	POST. REF.	DEBIT	CREDIT	BALANCE DEBIT	BALANCE CREDIT
20-- Dec.	31		G14		100.00		100.00
20-- Jan.	1		G15	100.00		—	—

ACCOUNT Income Summary ACCOUNT NO. 3120

DATE		ITEM	POST. REF.	DEBIT	CREDIT	BALANCE DEBIT	BALANCE CREDIT
20-- Dec.	31		G14	8,589.00		8,589.00	

ACCOUNT Interest Expense ACCOUNT NO. 8105

DATE		ITEM	POST. REF.	DEBIT	CREDIT	BALANCE DEBIT	BALANCE CREDIT
Dec.	31		CP21	160.00		8,489.00	
	31		G14	100.00		8,589.00	
	31		G14		8,589.00	—	—
20-- Jan.	1		G15		100.00		100.00
May	30		CP27	600.00		500.00	

Name ______________________ Date ______________ Class ______________

21-3 APPLICATION PROBLEM, pp. 629, 630

Journalizing and posting entries for accrued expenses

1.

Patti's Dress Shop

Work Sheet

For Year Ended December 31, 20 – –

	ACCOUNT TITLE	1 TRIAL BALANCE DEBIT	2 TRIAL BALANCE CREDIT	3 ADJUSTMENTS DEBIT	4 ADJUSTMENTS CREDIT
15	Interest Payable				(h) 260 00
51	Interest Expense	2,899 00		(h) 260 00	

2.

GENERAL JOURNAL PAGE 16

	DATE		ACCOUNT TITLE	DOC. NO.	POST. REF.	DEBIT	CREDIT	
1			*Adjusting Entries*					1
2	20-- *Dec.*	*31*	*Interest Expense*		*8105*	*260 00*		2
3			*Interest Payable*		*2110*		*260 00*	3
4								4
5			*Closing Entries*					5
6	20-- *Dec.*	*31*	*Income Summary*		*3120*	*3,159 00*		6
7			*Interest Expense*		*8105*		*3,159 00*	7
8								8

GENERAL JOURNAL PAGE 17

	DATE		ACCOUNT TITLE	DOC. NO.	POST. REF.	DEBIT	CREDIT	
1			*Reversing Entries*					1
2	20-- *Jan.*	*1*	*Interest Payable*		*2110*	*260 00*		2
3			*Interest Expense*		*8105*		*260 00*	3
4								4

3.

CASH PAYMENTS JOURNAL

PAGE 23

	DATE	ACCOUNT TITLE	CK. NO.	POST. REF.	1 GENERAL DEBIT	2 GENERAL CREDIT	3 ACCOUNTS PAYABLE DEBIT	4 PURCHASES DISCOUNT CREDIT	5 CASH CREDIT	
1	20-- Apr. 12	Notes Payable	377	2105	10 000 00				10 600 00	1
2		Interest Expense		8105	600 00					2
3										3
4										4
5										5
6										6
7										7
8										8
9										9
10										10
11										11
12										12
13										13
14										14
15										15
16										16
17										17
18										18
19										19
20										20
21										21
22										22
23										23
24										24

Name ______________________ Date ____________ Class ____________

21-3 APPLICATION PROBLEM (concluded)

2., 3.

GENERAL LEDGER

ACCOUNT Notes Payable — ACCOUNT NO. 2105

DATE		ITEM	POST. REF.	DEBIT	CREDIT	BALANCE DEBIT	BALANCE CREDIT
Oct.	14		CR11		10,000.00		10,000.00
20-- Apr.	12		CP23	10,000.00		—	—

ACCOUNT Interest Payable — ACCOUNT NO. 2110

DATE		ITEM	POST. REF.	DEBIT	CREDIT	BALANCE DEBIT	BALANCE CREDIT
20-- Dec.	31		G16		260.00		260.00
20-- Jan.	1		G17	260.00		—	—

ACCOUNT Income Summary — ACCOUNT NO. 3120

DATE		ITEM	POST. REF.	DEBIT	CREDIT	BALANCE DEBIT	BALANCE CREDIT
20-- Dec.	31		G16	3,159.00		3,159.00	

ACCOUNT Interest Expense — ACCOUNT NO. 8105

DATE		ITEM	POST. REF.	DEBIT	CREDIT	BALANCE DEBIT	BALANCE CREDIT
Dec.	31		CP19	80.00		2,899.00	
	31		G16	260.00		3,159.00	
	31		G16		3,159.00	—	—
20-- Jan.	1		G17		260.00		260.00
Apr.	12		CP23	600.00		340.00	

21-4 MASTERY PROBLEM, p. 630

Journalizing and posting entries for accrued interest revenue and expenses

1.

Youngblood, Inc.
Work Sheet
For Year Ended December 31, 20X1

	ACCOUNT TITLE	1 TRIAL BALANCE DEBIT	2 TRIAL BALANCE CREDIT	3 ADJUSTMENTS DEBIT	4 ADJUSTMENTS CREDIT
4	Interest Receivable			(a) 15 00	
15	Interest Payable				(h) 40 00
50	Interest Income		1,667 00		(a) 15 00
51	Interest Expense	2,732 00		(h) 40 00	

2., 3.

GENERAL JOURNAL — PAGE 15

	DATE		ACCOUNT TITLE	DOC. NO.	POST. REF.	DEBIT	CREDIT	
1			*Adjusting Entries*					1
2	20X1 Dec.	31	*Interest Receivable*		1120	15 00		2
3			*Interest Income*		7110		15 00	3
4		31	*Interest Expense*		8105	40 00		4
5			*Interest Payable*		2110		40 00	5
6								6
7			*Closing Entries*					7
8	20X1 Dec.	31	*Interest Income*		7110	1,682 00		8
9			*Income Summary*		3120		1,682 00	9
10		31	*Income Summary*		3120	2,772 00		10
11			*Interest Expense*		8105		2,772 00	11

4.

GENERAL JOURNAL — PAGE 16

	DATE		ACCOUNT TITLE	DOC. NO.	POST. REF.	DEBIT	CREDIT	
1			*Reversing Entries*					1
2	20X2 Jan.	1	*Interest Income*		7110	15 00		2
3			*Interest Receivable*		1120		15 00	3
4		1	*Interest Payable*		2110	40 00		4
5			*Interest Expense*		8105		40 00	5

Name ______________________ Date ______________ Class ______________

21-4 MASTERY PROBLEM (continued)

5.

CASH RECEIPTS JOURNAL PAGE 16

	DATE		ACCOUNT TITLE	DOC. NO.	POST. REF.	1 GENERAL DEBIT	2 GENERAL CREDIT	3 ACCOUNTS RECEIVABLE CREDIT	4 SALES CREDIT	5 SALES TAX PAYABLE CREDIT	6 SALES DISCOUNT DEBIT	7 CASH DEBIT	
1	20X2 Feb.	9	Notes Receivable	R336	1115		9000 00					9270 00	1
2			Interest Income		7110		270 00						2
3													3
4													4
5													5
6													6
7													7
8													8

6.

CASH PAYMENTS JOURNAL PAGE 28

	DATE		ACCOUNT TITLE	CK. NO.	POST. REF.	1 GENERAL DEBIT	2 GENERAL CREDIT	3 ACCOUNTS PAYABLE DEBIT	4 PURCHASES DISCOUNT CREDIT	5 CASH CREDIT	
1	20X2 Apr.	5	Notes Payable	612	2105	7200 00				7392 00	1
2			Interest Expense		8105	192 00					2
3											3
4											4
5											5
6											6

21-4 MASTERY PROBLEM (continued)

2., 3., 4., 5., 6.

GENERAL LEDGER

ACCOUNT Notes Receivable — ACCOUNT NO. 1115

DATE		ITEM	POST. REF.	DEBIT	CREDIT	BALANCE DEBIT	BALANCE CREDIT
Nov.	11		G12	900 00		900 00	
20X2 Feb.	9		CR16		900 00	—	—

ACCOUNT Interest Receivable — ACCOUNT NO. 1120

DATE		ITEM	POST. REF.	DEBIT	CREDIT	BALANCE DEBIT	BALANCE CREDIT
20X1 Dec.	31		G15	15 00		15 00	
20X2 Jan.	1		G16		15 00	—	—

ACCOUNT Notes Payable — ACCOUNT NO. 2105

DATE		ITEM	POST. REF.	DEBIT	CREDIT	BALANCE DEBIT	BALANCE CREDIT
Dec.	6		CR12		7,200 00		7,200 00
20X2 Apr.	5		CP28	7,200 00		—	—

ACCOUNT Interest Payable — ACCOUNT NO. 2110

DATE		ITEM	POST. REF.	DEBIT	CREDIT	BALANCE DEBIT	BALANCE CREDIT
20X1 Dec.	31		G15		40 00		40 00
20X2 Jan.	1		G16	40 00		—	—

Name ______ Date ______ Class ______

21-4 MASTERY PROBLEM (concluded)

2., 3., 4., 5., 6. **GENERAL LEDGER**

ACCOUNT Income Summary ACCOUNT NO. 3120

DATE		ITEM	POST. REF.	DEBIT	CREDIT	BALANCE DEBIT	BALANCE CREDIT
20X1 Dec.	31		G15		1,682.00		1,682.00
	31		G15	2,772.00		1,090.00	

ACCOUNT Interest Income ACCOUNT NO. 7110

DATE		ITEM	POST. REF.	DEBIT	CREDIT	BALANCE DEBIT	BALANCE CREDIT
Dec.	31		CR14		32.00		1,667.00
	31		G15		15.00		1,682.00
	31		G15	1,682.00		—	—
20X2 Jan.	1		G16	15.00		15.00	
Feb.	9		CR16		27.00		12.00

ACCOUNT Interest Expense ACCOUNT NO. 8105

DATE		ITEM	POST. REF.	DEBIT	CREDIT	BALANCE DEBIT	BALANCE CREDIT
Dec.	31		CP21	87.50		2,732.00	
	31		G15	40.00		2,772.00	
	31		G15		2,772.00	—	—
20X2 Jan.	1		G16		40.00		40.00
Apr.	5		CP28	192.00		152.00	

21-5 CHALLENGE PROBLEM, pp. 630, 631

Journalizing and posting entries for accrued interest revenue and expenses

1.

Blackwell Corporation
Work Sheet
For Year Ended December 31, 20X1

	ACCOUNT TITLE	TRIAL BALANCE DEBIT (1)	TRIAL BALANCE CREDIT (2)	ADJUSTMENTS DEBIT (3)	ADJUSTMENTS CREDIT (4)
4	Interest Receivable			(a) 10 35	
15	Interest Payable				(h) 53 33
50	Interest Income		1 897 00		(a) 10 35
51	Interest Expense	1 648 00		(h) 53 33	

2.

GENERAL JOURNAL PAGE 16

	DATE		ACCOUNT TITLE	DOC. NO.	POST. REF.	DEBIT	CREDIT	
1			*Adjusting Entries*					1
2	20X1 Dec.	31	*Interest Receivable*		1120	10 35		2
3			*Interest Income*		7110		10 35	3
4		31	*Interest Expense*		8105	53 33		4
5			*Interest Payable*		2110		53 33	5
6								6
7			*Closing Entries*					7
8	20X1 Dec.	31	*Interest Income*		7110	1 907 35		8
9			*Income Summary*		3120		1 907 35	9
10		31	*Income Summary*		3120	1 701 33		10
11			*Interest Expense*		8105		1 701 33	11

GENERAL JOURNAL PAGE 17

	DATE		ACCOUNT TITLE	DOC. NO.	POST. REF.	DEBIT	CREDIT	
1			*Reversing Entries*					1
2	20X2 Jan.	1	*Interest Income*		7110	10 35		2
3			*Interest Receivable*		1120		10 35	3
4		1	*Interest Payable*		2110	53 33		4
5			*Interest Expense*		8105		53 33	5

21-5 CHALLENGE PROBLEM (continued)

3.

GENERAL JOURNAL

PAGE 18

	DATE		ACCOUNT TITLE	DOC. NO.	POST. REF.	DEBIT	CREDIT	
1	20X2 Mar.	8	Accounts Receivable/Margaret Snider	M98	✓	940 50		1
2			Notes Receivable		1115		900 00	2
3			Interest Income		7110		40 50	3
4								4
5								5

CASH PAYMENTS JOURNAL

PAGE 15

	DATE		ACCOUNT TITLE	CK. NO.	POST. REF.	1 GENERAL DEBIT	2 GENERAL CREDIT	3 ACCOUNTS PAYABLE DEBIT	4 PURCHASES DISCOUNT CREDIT	5 CASH CREDIT	
1	20X2 Mar.	12	Notes Payable	645	2105	10,000 00				10,290 00	1
2			Interest Expense		8105	290 00					2
3											3
4											4
5											5
6											6
7											7
8											8
9											9
10											10
11											11
12											12

2., 3.

GENERAL LEDGER

ACCOUNT Notes Receivable — ACCOUNT NO. 1115

DATE		ITEM	POST. REF.	DEBIT	CREDIT	BALANCE DEBIT	BALANCE CREDIT
Dec.	8		G14	900 00		900 00	
20X2 Mar.	8		G18		900 00	—	—

ACCOUNT Interest Receivable — ACCOUNT NO. 1120

DATE		ITEM	POST. REF.	DEBIT	CREDIT	BALANCE DEBIT	BALANCE CREDIT
20X1 Dec.	31		G16	10 35		10 35	
20X2 Jan.	1		G17		10 35	—	—

ACCOUNT Notes Payable — ACCOUNT NO. 2105

DATE		ITEM	POST. REF.	DEBIT	CREDIT	BALANCE DEBIT	BALANCE CREDIT
Dec.	15		CR12		10 000 00		10 000 00
20X2 Mar.	12		CP15	10 000 00		—	—

ACCOUNT Interest Payable — ACCOUNT NO. 2110

DATE		ITEM	POST. REF.	DEBIT	CREDIT	BALANCE DEBIT	BALANCE CREDIT
20X1 Dec.	31		G16		53 33		53 33
20X2 Jan.	1		G17	53 33		—	—

21-5 CHALLENGE PROBLEM (concluded)

2., 3.

GENERAL LEDGER

ACCOUNT Income Summary — ACCOUNT NO. 3120

DATE		ITEM	POST. REF.	DEBIT	CREDIT	BALANCE DEBIT	BALANCE CREDIT
20X1 Dec.	31		G16		1,907.35		1,907.35
	31		G16	1,701.33			206.02

ACCOUNT Interest Income — ACCOUNT NO. 7110

DATE		ITEM	POST. REF.	DEBIT	CREDIT	BALANCE DEBIT	BALANCE CREDIT
Dec.	31		CR12		85.00		1,897.00
	31		G16		10.35		1,907.35
	31		G16	1,907.35		—	—
20X2 Jan.	1		G17	10.35		10.35	
Mar.	8		G18		40.50		30.15

ACCOUNT Interest Expense — ACCOUNT NO. 8105

DATE		ITEM	POST. REF.	DEBIT	CREDIT	BALANCE DEBIT	BALANCE CREDIT
Dec.	31		CP12	100.00		1,648.00	
	31		G16	53.33		1,701.33	
	31		G16		1,701.33	—	—
20X2 Jan.	1		G17		53.33		53.33
Mar.	12		CP15	290.00		236.67	

Study Guide 22

Name	Perfect Score	Your Score
Identifying Accounting Concepts and Practices for End-of-Fiscal-Period Work	20 Pts.	
Analyzing End-of-Fiscal-Period Entries for a Corporation	34 Pts.	
Total	54 Pts.	

Part One—Identifying Accounting Concepts and Practices for End-of-Fiscal-Period Work

Directions: Place a *T* for True or an *F* for False in the Answers column to show whether each of the following statements is true or false.

	Answers
1. Financial statements are prepared using a completed work sheet. (p. 636)	1. *T*
2. Businesses use work sheets to plan adjustments and provide information needed to prepare financial statements. (p. 636)	2. *T*
3. All accounts that need to be brought up to date are adjusted after financial statements are prepared. (p. 637)	3. *F*
4. To adjust the interest income earned during the current fiscal period but not yet received, the Interest Receivable account is debited. (p. 638)	4. *T*
5. To bring the Supplies account up to date, the balance of supplies needs to be decreased by the cost of supplies used during the year. (p. 638)	5. *T*
6. Federal income tax is an expense of a corporation. (p. 639)	6. *T*
7. The tax rate for federal income tax varies depending on the amount of net income earned. (p. 639)	7. *T*
8. Corporations with less than $50,000 net income pay smaller tax rates than corporations with larger net incomes. (p. 640)	8. *T*
9. When the total of a work sheet's Income Statement Credit column is larger than the total of the Income Statement Debit column, the difference represents net loss of the business. (p. 641)	9. *F*
10. A work sheet's Balance Sheet columns are used to calculate net income after federal income tax. (p. 641)	10. *F*
11. The balance of Capital Stock is recorded in the Income Statement columns of a work sheet. (p. 642)	11. *F*
12. A corporation's preparation of financial statements to report the financial progress during a fiscal period is an application of the Accounting Period Cycle concept. (p. 646)	12. *T*
13. To calculate the component percentage of cost of merchandise sold, divide net sales by cost of merchandise sold. (p. 647)	13. *F*
14. A statement of stockholders' equity contains two major sections: capital stock and retained earnings. (p. 649)	14. *T*
15. The book value of an asset is reported on a balance sheet by listing two amounts: the balance of the asset account and the balance of the asset's contra account. (p. 651)	15. *F*
16. An example of a long-term liability is Mortgage Payable. (p. 651)	16. *T*
17. A business can use the amount of working capital to provide a convenient relative measurement from year to year. (p. 652)	17. *F*

	Answers
18. Closing entries for a corporation are made from information in a balance sheet. (p. 655)	**18.** *F*
19. Dividends increase the earnings retained by a corporation. (p. 657)	**19.** *F*
20. A reversing entry is desirable if an adjusting entry creates a balance in an asset or a liability account. (p. 658)	**20.** *T*

Name ______________________ Date ______________ Class ______________

Part Two—Analyzing End-of-Fiscal-Period Entries for a Corporation

Directions: For each closing or reversing entry described, decide which accounts are debited and credited. Print the letter identifying your choice in the proper Answers columns. (Accounts are listed in alphabetical order.)

Account Titles

A. Cash Short and Over
B. Depreciation Expense —Store Equipment
C. Dividends
D. Dividends Payable
E. Federal Income Tax Expense
F. Federal Income Tax Payable
G. Gain on Plant Assets
H. Income Summary
I. Insurance Expense
J. Interest Expense
K. Interest Income
L. Interest Payable
M. Interest Receivable
N. Loss on Plant Assets
O. Purchases
P. Purchases Discount
Q. Purchases Returns and Allowances
R. Retained Earnings
S. Sales
T. Sales Discount

Transactions	Answers Debit	Answers Credit
1–2. Closing entry for the sales account. (p. 655)	1. *S*	2. *H*
3–4. Closing entry for purchases discount. (p. 655)	3. *P*	4. *H*
5–6. Closing entry for the purchases returns and allowances account. (p. 655)	5. *Q*	6. *H*
7–8. Closing entry for the gain on plant assets account. (p. 655)	7. *G*	8. *H*
9–10. Closing entry for the interest income account. (p. 655)	9. *K*	10. *H*
11–12. Closing entry for the sales discount account. (p. 656)	11. *H*	12. *T*
13–14. Closing entry for the purchases account. (p. 656)	13. *H*	14. *O*
15–16. Closing entry for the cash short and over account (cash is short). (p. 656)	15. *H*	16. *A*
17–18. Closing entry for the cash short and over account (cash is over). (p. 656)	17. *A*	18. *H*
19–20. Closing entry for the depreciation expense—store equipment account. (p. 656)	19. *H*	20. *B*
21–22. Closing entry for the federal income tax expense account. (p. 656)	21. *H*	22. *E*
23–24. Closing entry for the income summary account (net income). (p. 657)	23. *H*	24. *R*
25–26. Closing entry for the income summary account (net loss). (p. 657)	25. *R*	26. *H*
27–28. Closing entry for the dividends account. (p. 657)	27. *R*	28. *C*
29–30. Reversing entry for the accrued interest income account. (p. 658)	29. *K*	30. *M*
31–32. Reversing entry for the accrued interest expense. (p. 658)	31. *L*	32. *J*
33–34. Reversing entry for the federal income tax payable account. (p. 658)	33. *F*	34. *E*

Study Skills

Estimating Math Answers

Being able to estimate math answers quickly is advantageous for everyone. When you go shopping, do you know approximately how much your bill is going to be before you check out? Before you work out a math problem at school, do you know about what the answer should be?

Make a Good Guess

Being able to estimate answers will help you at school. Suppose you want to average 10 grades ranging from 90 to 100. You should be able to estimate that the total of the 10 grades should be about 950, and the average should be about 95. If your answer is 70 when you calculate the average, you know immediately that the answer is not sensible.

Avoid Errors Using Decimal Places

Students sometimes place a decimal in the wrong place in the answer to a math problem. This is an error that you will not make if you know approximately how much the answer should be before you begin figuring.

This may sound surprising, but students sometimes make an error similar to the following. The teacher asks what is 10 percent of $100, and the student answers $1,000.

Any student who takes a few seconds to think about the problem will know immediately that the answer is smaller, not larger, than the original $100. By estimating the answer first, you can avoid making what appears to be a ridiculous error.

Dependence on the Calculator

The pocket calculator is a wonderful device. It can save you a great amount of time when you must do a math problem. However, you must not let yourself become so dependent on a calculator that you make errors simply because you do not estimate answers.

A Sensible Approach

Being able to estimate math answers can help you every day. Before you begin calculating, ask yourself what a sensible answer would be. If the final answer is not reasonably close to your estimate, you have very likely made an error. A little practice can save you money when you shop and improve your grades at school.

[This page left blank intentionally.]

22-1 WORK TOGETHER, p. 644

Preparing a work sheet for a corporation

1., 2.

Webster Corporation

Work Sheet

For Year Ended December 31, 20 – –

	ACCOUNT TITLE	1 TRIAL BALANCE DEBIT	2 TRIAL BALANCE CREDIT	3 ADJUSTMENTS DEBIT	4 ADJUSTMENTS CREDIT	5 INCOME STATEMENT DEBIT	6 INCOME STATEMENT CREDIT	7 BALANCE SHEET DEBIT	8 BALANCE SHEET CREDIT	
1	Cash	90,052.23						90,052.23		1
2	Petty Cash	300.00						300.00		2
3	Notes Receivable	10,952.00						10,952.00		3
4	Interest Receivable			(a) 275.00				275.00		4
5	Accounts Receivable	70,094.10						70,094.10		5
6	Allowance for Uncoll. Accts.		44.64		(b) 7,350.00				7,394.64	6
7	Merchandise Inventory	64,316.30		(c) 25,800.00				90,116.30		7
8	Supplies	2,552.08			(d) 2,300.00			252.08		8
9	Prepaid Insurance	9,071.60			(e) 6,000.00			3,071.60		9
10	Office Equipment	27,940.00						27,940.00		10
11	Accum. Depr.—Office Equip.		6,735.00		(f) 2,800.00				9,535.00	11
12	Store Equipment	22,199.20						22,199.20		12
13	Accum. Depr.—Store Equip.		6,357.40		(g) 1,700.60				8,058.00	13
14	Notes Payable		14,400.00						14,400.00	14
15	Interest Payable				(h) 555.16				555.16	15
16	Accounts Payable		60,116.18						60,116.18	16
17	Employee Inc. Tax Payable		1,652.40						1,652.40	17
18	Federal Inc. Tax Payable				(i) 1,752.70				1,752.70	18
19	Social Security Tax Payable		1,549.19						1,549.19	19
20	Medicare Tax Payable		357.51						357.51	20
21	Sales Tax Payable		6,652.60						6,652.60	21
22	Unemploy. Tax Pay.—Fed.		33.44						33.44	22
23	Unemploy. Tax Pay.—State		225.72						225.72	23
24	Health Ins. Premiums Pay.		702.60						702.60	24
25	Dividends Payable		10,800.00						10,800.00	25
26	Capital Stock		100,000.00						100,000.00	26
27	Retained Earnings		59,241.54						59,241.54	27
28	Dividends	43,200.00						43,200.00		28
29	Income Summary				(c) 25,800.00		25,800.00			29
30	Sales		1075,868.30				1075,868.30			30
31	Sales Discount	2,020.80				2,020.80				31
32	Sales Ret. and Allowances	8,347.20				8,347.20				32

Total of Income Statement Credit column	$1,111,147.52
Less total of Income Statement Debit column before federal income tax	−1,014,668.99
Equals Net Income before Federal Income Tax	$ 96,478.53

22-1 WORK TOGETHER (concluded)

Webster Corporation

Work Sheet (continued)

For Year Ended December 31, 20 – –

	Account Title	1 Trial Balance Debit	2 Trial Balance Credit	3 Adjustments Debit	4 Adjustments Credit	5 Income Statement Debit	6 Income Statement Credit	7 Balance Sheet Debit	8 Balance Sheet Credit	
33	Purchases	737,464.80				737,464.80				33
34	Purchases Discount		5,483.60				5,483.60			34
35	Purchases Ret. and Allow.		2,716.14				2,716.14			35
36	Advertising Expense	15,947.00				15,947.00				36
37	Cash Short and Over	9.15				9.15				37
38	Credit Card Fee Expense	10,066.94				10,066.94				38
39	Depr. Exp.—Office Equip.			(f) 2,800.00		2,800.00				39
40	Depr. Exp.—Store Equip.			(g) 1,700.60		1,700.60				40
41	Insurance Expense			(e) 6,000.00		6,000.00				41
42	Miscellaneous Expense	8,682.20				8,682.20				42
43	Payroll Taxes Expense	14,966.00				14,966.00				43
44	Rent Expense	28,915.00				28,915.00				44
45	Repair Expense	3,485.00				3,485.00				45
46	Salary Expense	158,964.00				158,964.00				46
47	Supplies Expense			(d) 2,300.00		2,300.00				47
48	Uncollectible Accounts Exp.			(b) 7,350.00		7,350.00				48
49	Utilities Expense	2,661.00				2,661.00				49
50	Gain on Plant Assets		110.00				110.00			50
51	Interest Income		894.48		(a) 275.00		1,169.48			51
52	Interest Expense	2,186.14		(h) 555.16		2,741.30				52
53	Loss on Plant Assets	248.00				248.00				53
54	Federal Income Tax Expense	19,300.00		(i) 1,752.70		21,052.70				54
55		1,353,940.74	1,353,940.74	48,533.46	48,533.46	1,035,721.69	1,111,147.52	358,452.51	283,026.68	55
56	Net Inc. after Fed. Inc. Tax					75,425.83			75,425.83	56
57						1,111,147.52	1,111,147.52	358,452.51	358,452.51	57
58										58
59										59
60										60
61										61
62										62

Net Income before Taxes	×	Tax Rate	=	Federal Income Tax Amount
$50,000.00	×	15%	=	$ 7,500.00
Plus 25,000.00	×	25%	=	6,250.00
Plus $21,478.53	×	34%	=	7,302.70
Plus	×	39%	=	
Total $96,478.53				$21,052.70

22-1 ON YOUR OWN, p. 644

Preparing a work sheet for a corporation

1., 2.

Osborn Corporation

Work Sheet

For Year Ended December 31, 20 – –

	ACCOUNT TITLE	1 TRIAL BALANCE DEBIT	2 TRIAL BALANCE CREDIT	3 ADJUSTMENTS DEBIT	4 ADJUSTMENTS CREDIT	5 INCOME STATEMENT DEBIT	6 INCOME STATEMENT CREDIT	7 BALANCE SHEET DEBIT	8 BALANCE SHEET CREDIT	
1	Cash	6848 00						6848 00		1
2	Petty Cash	300 00						300 00		2
3	Notes Receivable	8000 00						8000 00		3
4	Interest Receivable			(a) 160 00				160 00		4
5	Accounts Receivable	82483 22						82483 22		5
6	Allowance for Uncoll. Accts.		280 00		(b) 7312 00				7592 00	6
7	Merchandise Inventory	195884 25		(c) 2108 01				197992 26		7
8	Supplies	9218 25			(d) 8415 75			802 50		8
9	Prepaid Insurance	15800 00			(e) 14600 00			1200 00		9
10	Office Equipment	35188 50						35188 50		10
11	Accum. Depr.—Office Equip.		22188 50		(f) 6440 00				28628 50	11
12	Store Equipment	43884 25						43884 25		12
13	Accum. Depr.—Store Equip.		28178 00		(g) 8250 00				36428 00	13
14	Notes Payable		9000 00						9000 00	14
15	Interest Payable				(h) 300 00				300 00	15
16	Accounts Payable		18489 25						18489 25	16
17	Employee Inc. Tax Payable		2256 00						2256 00	17
18	Federal Inc. Tax Payable				(i) 5296 94				5296 94	18
19	Social Security Tax Payable		2121 34						2121 34	19
20	Medicare Tax Payable		512 66						512 66	20
21	Sales Tax Payable		5976 00						5976 00	21
22	Unemploy. Tax Pay.—Fed.		45 60						45 60	22
23	Unemploy. Tax Pay.—State		292 80						292 80	23
24	Health Ins. Premiums Pay.		672 00						672 00	24
25	Dividends Payable		5000 00						5000 00	25
26	Capital Stock		50000 00						50000 00	26
27	Retained Earnings		54142 16						54142 16	27
28	Dividends	20000 00						20000 00		28

Total of Income Statement Credit column	$2,603,873.63
Less total of Income Statement Debit column before federal income tax	–2,352,471.21
Equals Net Income before Federal Income Tax	$ 251,402.42

Name ______________________ Date ______________ Class ______________

22-1 ON YOUR OWN (concluded)

Osborn Corporation

Work Sheet (continued)

For Year Ended December 31, 20 – –

	Account Title	1 Trial Balance Debit	2 Trial Balance Credit	3 Adjustments Debit	4 Adjustments Credit	5 Income Statement Debit	6 Income Statement Credit	7 Balance Sheet Debit	8 Balance Sheet Credit	
29	Income Summary				(c) 2,108.01		2,108.01			29
30	Sales		2,584,483.25				2,584,483.25			30
31	Sales Discount	12,485.28				12,485.28				31
32	Sales Returns and Allow.	22,894.10				22,894.10				32
33	Purchases	1,638,817.14				1,638,817.14				33
34	Purchases Discount		7,891.17				7,891.17			34
35	Purchases Ret. and Allow.		6,148.20				6,148.20			35
36	Advertising Expense	38,114.20				38,114.20				36
37	Cash Short and Over	153.33				153.33				37
38	Credit Card Fee Expense	18,122.10				18,122.10				38
39	Depr. Exp.—Office Equip.			(f) 6,440.00		6,440.00				39
40	Depr. Exp.—Store Equip.			(g) 8,250.00		8,250.00				40
41	Insurance Expense			(e) 14,600.00		14,600.00				41
42	Miscellaneous Expense	29,485.25				29,485.25				42
43	Payroll Taxes Expense	32,148.24				32,148.24				43
44	Rent Expense	54,000.00				54,000.00				44
45	Repair Expense	12,487.93				12,487.93				45
46	Salary Expense	421,584.99				421,584.99				46
47	Supplies Expense			(d) 8,415.75		8,415.75				47
48	Uncollectible Accounts Exp.			(b) 7,312.00		7,312.00				48
49	Utilities Expense	23,199.90				23,199.90				49
50	Gain on Plant Assets		2,458.00				2,458.00			50
51	Interest Income		625.00		(a) 160.00		785.00			51
52	Interest Expense	1,780.00		(h) 300.00		2,080.00				52
53	Loss on Plant Assets	2,019.00				2,019.00				53
54	Federal Income Tax Expense	76,000.00		(i) 5,296.94		81,296.94				54
55		2,800,759.93	2,800,759.93	52,882.70	52,882.70	2,433,768.15	2,603,873.63	396,858.73	226,753.25	55
56	Net Inc. after Fed. Inc. Tax					170,105.48			170,105.48	56
57						2,603,873.63	2,603,873.63	396,858.73	396,858.73	57

Net Income before Taxes	×	Tax Rate	=	Federal Income Tax Amount
$ 50,000.00	×	15%	=	$ 7,500.00
Plus 25,000.00	×	25%	=	6,250.00
Plus 25,000.00	×	34%	=	8,500.00
Plus 151,402.42	×	39%	=	59,046.94
Total $251,402.42				$81,296.94

22-2 WORK TOGETHER, p. 648

Preparing an income statement for a corporation

1.

Webster Corporation

Income Statement

For Year Ended December 31, 20 – –

					% OF NET SALES
Operating Revenue:					
Sales			1,075,868.30		
Less: Sales Discount		2,020.80			
Sales Returns and Allowances		8,347.20	10,368.00		
Net Sales				1,065,500.30	100.0
Cost of Merchandise Sold:					
Merchandise Inventory, Jan. 1, 20 – –			64,316.30		
Purchases		737,464.80			
Less: Purchases Discount	5,483.60				
Purchases Ret. and Allow.	2,716.14	8,199.74			
Net Purchases			729,265.06		
Total Cost of Mdse. Avail. for Sale			793,581.36		
Less Mdse. Inventory, Dec. 31, 20 – –			90,116.30		
Cost of Merchandise Sold				703,465.06	66.0
Gross Profit on Operations				362,035.24	34.0
Operating Expenses:					
Advertising Expense			15,947.00		
Cash Short and Over			9.15		
Credit Card Fee Expense			10,066.94		
Depr. Expense—Office Equipment			2,800.00		
Depr. Expense—Store Equipment			1,700.60		
Insurance Expense			6,000.00		
Miscellaneous Expense			8,682.20		
Payroll Taxes Expense			14,966.00		
Rent Expense			28,915.00		
Repair Expense			3,485.00		
Salary Expense			158,964.00		
Supplies Expense			2,300.00		
Uncollectible Accounts Expense			7,350.00		
Utilities Expense			2,661.00		
Total Operating Expenses				263,846.89	24.8
Income from Operations				98,188.35	9.2

Name ______________________ Date ____________ Class ____________

22-2 WORK TOGETHER (concluded)

1.

Webster Corporation

Income Statement (continued)

For Year Ended December 31, 20 – –

					% OF NET SALES
Other Revenue:					
Gain on Plant Assets		110.00			
Interest Income		1,169.48			
Total Other Revenue			1,279.48		
Other Expenses:					
Interest Expense		2,741.30			
Loss on Plant Assets		248.00			
Total Other Expenses			2,989.30		
Net Deduction				1,709.82	0.2
Net Income before Fed. Income Tax				96,478.53	9.1
Less Federal Income Tax Expense				21,052.70	
Net Income after Federal Income Tax				75,425.83	

2.

	Acceptable %	Actual %	Positive Result: Yes	Positive Result: No	Recommended Action If Needed
Cost of merchandise sold	Not more than 68.0%	*66.0%*	✓		*None*
Gross profit on operations	Not less than 32.0%	*34.0%*	✓		*None*
Total operating expenses	Not more than 22.0%	*24.8%*		✓	*Review and identify excessive expenses so they may be controlled.*
Income from operations	Not less than 10.0%	*9.2%*		✓	*Controlling expenses will raise this percentage above the acceptable level.*
Net deduction from other revenue and expenses	Not more than 0.1%	*0.2%*		✓	*Review interest expense transactions and pursue ways of reducing the cost of long-term borrowing.*
Net income before federal income tax	Not less than 9.8%	*9.1%*		✓	*Controlling expenses will raise this percentage above the acceptable level.*

22-2 ON YOUR OWN, p. 648

Preparing an income statement for a corporation

1.

Osborn Corporation

Income Statement

For Year Ended December 31, 20 – –

					% OF NET SALES
Operating Revenue:					
Sales			2,584,483.25		
Less: Sales Discount		12,485.28			
Sales Returns and Allowances		22,894.10	35,379.38		
Net Sales				2,549,103.87	100.0
Cost of Merchandise Sold:					
Merchandise Inventory, Jan. 1, 20 – –			195,884.25		
Purchases		1,638,817.14			
Less: Purchases Discount	7,891.17				
Purchases Ret. and Allow.	6,148.20	14,039.37			
Net Purchases			1,624,777.77		
Total Cost of Mdse. Avail. for Sale			1,820,662.02		
Less Mdse. Inventory, Dec. 31, 20 – –			197,992.26		
Cost of Merchandise Sold				1,622,669.76	63.7
Gross Profit on Operations				926,434.11	36.3
Operating Expenses:					
Advertising Expense			38,114.20		
Cash Short and Over			15.33		
Credit Card Fee Expense			18,122.10		
Depr. Expense—Office Equipment			6,440.00		
Depr. Expense—Store Equipment			8,250.00		
Insurance Expense			14,600.00		
Miscellaneous Expense			29,485.25		
Payroll Taxes Expense			32,148.24		
Rent Expense			54,000.00		
Repair Expense			12,487.93		
Salary Expense			421,584.99		
Supplies Expense			8,415.75		
Uncollectible Accounts Expense			7,312.00		
Utilities Expense			23,199.90		
Total Operating Expenses				674,175.69	26.4
Income from Operations				252,258.42	9.9

Name ______________________ Date ______________ Class ______________

22-2 ON YOUR OWN (concluded)

1.

Osborn Corporation

Income Statement (continued)

For Year Ended December 31, 20 – –

					% OF NET SALES
Other Revenue:					
Gain on Plant Assets		2,458.00			
Interest Income		785.00			
Total Other Income			3,243.00		
Other Expenses:					
Interest Expense		2,080.00			
Loss on Plant Assets		2,019.00			
Total Other Expenses			4,099.00		
Net Deduction				856.00	0.0
Net Income before Fed. Income Tax				251,402.42	9.9
Less Federal Income Tax Expense				81,296.94	
Net Income after Federal Income Tax				170,105.48	

	Acceptable %	Actual %	Positive Result Yes	Positive Result No	Recommended Action If Needed
Cost of merchandise sold	Not more than 60.0%	*63.7%*		✓	*Identify ways of reducing the cost of merchandise or increase the unit sales price of merchandise.*
Gross profit on operations	Not less than 40.0%	*36.3%*		✓	*Changes in purchasing or pricing policies will increase this percentage.*
Total operating expenses	Not more than 28.0%	*26.4%*	✓		*None*
Income from operations	Not less than 12.0%	*9.9%*		✓	*Changes in purchasing or pricing policies will increase this percentage.*
Net deduction from other revenue and expenses	Not more than 0.1%	*0.0%*	✓		*None*
Net income before federal income tax	Not less than 11.9%	*9.9%*		✓	*Changes in purchasing or pricing policies and controlling interest expenses will increase this percentage.*

22-3 WORK TOGETHER, p. 653

Preparing a statement of stockholders' equity and balance sheet for a corporation

1.

Webster Corporation

Statement of Stockholders' Equity

For Year Ended December 31, 20 – –

Capital Stock:			
$10.00 Par Value			
January 1, 20 – –, 9,000 Shares Issued		90 000 00	
Issued during Current Year, 1,000 Shares		10 000 00	
Balance, December 31, 20 – –, 10,000 Shares Issued			100 000 00
Retained Earnings:			
Balance, January 1, 20 – –		59 241 54	
Net Income after Federal Income Tax for 20 – –	75 425 83		
Less Dividends Declared during 20 – –	43 200 00		
Net Increase during 20 – –		32 225 83	
Balance, December 31, 20 – –			91 467 37
Total Stockholders' Equity, December 31, 20 – –			191 467 37

22-3 WORK TOGETHER (continued)

2.

Webster Corporation

Balance Sheet

December 31, 20 – –

Assets			
Current Assets:			
Cash		90,052.23	
Petty Cash		300.00	
Notes Receivable		10,952.00	
Interest Receivable		275.00	
Accounts Receivable	70,094.10		
Less Allowance for Uncollectible Accounts	7,394.64	62,699.46	
Merchandise Inventory		90,116.30	
Supplies		252.08	
Prepaid Insurance		3,071.60	
Total Current Assets			257,718.67
Plant Assets:			
Office Equipment	27,940.00		
Less Accumulated Depreciation—Office Equipment	9,535.00	18,405.00	
Store Equipment	22,199.20		
Less Accumulated Depreciation—Store Equipment	8,058.00	14,141.20	
Total Plant Assets			32,546.20
Total Assets			290,264.87
Liabilities			
Current Liabilities:			
Notes Payable		14,400.00	
Interest Payable		555.16	
Accounts Payable		60,116.18	
Employee Income Tax Payable		1,652.40	
Federal Income Tax Payable		1,752.70	
Social Security Tax Payable		1,549.19	
Medicare Tax Payable		357.51	
Sales Tax Payable		6,652.60	
Unemployment Tax Payable—Federal		33.44	
Unemployment Tax Payable—State		225.72	
Health Insurance Premiums Payable		702.60	
Dividends Payable		10,800.00	
Total Liabilities			98,797.50

2.

Webster Corporation

Balance Sheet (continued)

December 31, 20 – –

Stockholders' Equity			
Capital Stock		100 000 00	
Retained Earnings		91 467 37	
Total Stockholders' Equity			191 467 37
Total Liabilities and Stockholders' Equity			290 264 87

3., 4.

	Acceptable	Actual	Positive Result Yes	Positive Result No	Recommended Action If Needed
Working capital	Not less than $150,000	*$158,921.17*	✓		*None*
Current ratio	Between 2.0 to 1 and 3.0 to 1	*2.61 to 1*	✓		*None*

Name ______________________ Date ______________ Class ______________

22-3 ON YOUR OWN, p. 653

Preparing a statement of stockholders' equity and balance sheet for a corporation

1.

Osborn Corporation

Statement of Stockholders' Equity

For Year Ended December 31, 20 – –

Capital Stock:			
$1.00 Per Share			
January 1, 20 – –, 45,000 Shares Issued		45 000 00	
Issued during Current Year, 5,000 Shares		5 000 00	
Balance, December 31, 20 – –, 50,000 Shares Issued			50 000 00
Retained Earnings:			
Balance, January 1, 20 – –		54 142 16	
Net Income after Federal Income Tax for 20 – –	170 105 48		
Less Dividends Declared during 20 – –	20 000 00		
Net Increase during 20 – –		150 105 48	
Balance, December 31, 20 – –			204 247 64
Total Stockholders' Equity, December 31, 20 – –			254 247 64

2.

Osborn Corporation

Balance Sheet

December 31, 20 – –

Assets			
Current Assets:			
Cash		6,848.00	
Petty Cash		300.00	
Notes Receivable		8,000.00	
Interest Receivable		160.00	
Accounts Receivable	82,483.22		
Less Allowance for Uncollectible Accounts	7,592.00	74,891.22	
Merchandise Inventory		197,992.26	
Supplies		802.50	
Prepaid Insurance		1,200.00	
Total Current Assets			290,193.98
Plant Assets:			
Office Equipment	35,188.50		
Less Accumulated Depreciation—Office Equipment	28,628.50	6,560.00	
Store Equipment	43,884.25		
Less Accumulated Depreciation—Store Equipment	36,428.00	7,456.25	
Total Plant Assets			14,016.25
Total Assets			304,210.23
Liabilities			
Current Liabilities:			
Notes Payable		9,000.00	
Interest Payable		300.00	
Accounts Payable		18,489.25	
Employee Income Tax Payable		2,256.00	
Federal Income Tax Payable		5,296.94	
Social Security Tax Payable		2,121.34	
Medicare Tax Payable		512.66	
Sales Tax Payable		5,976.00	
Unemployment Tax Payable—Federal		45.60	
Unemployment Tax Payable—State		292.80	
Health Insurance Premiums Payable		672.00	
Dividends Payable		5,000.00	
Total Liabilities			49,962.59
Stockholders' Equity			
Capital Stock		50,000.00	
Retained Earnings		204,247.64	
Total Stockholders' Equity			254,247.64
Total Liabilities and Stockholders' Equity			304,210.23

22-3 ON YOUR OWN (concluded)

3., 4.

	Acceptable	Actual	Positive Result		Recommended Action If Needed
			Yes	No	
Working capital	Not less than $100,000	***$240,231.39***	✓		***None***
Current ratio	Between 5.0 to 1 and 6.0 to 1	***5.81 to 1***	✓		***None***

Journalizing adjusting, closing, and reversing entries for a corporation

1.

GENERAL JOURNAL PAGE 15

	DATE		ACCOUNT TITLE	DOC. NO.	POST. REF.	DEBIT	CREDIT	
1			*Adjusting Entries*					1
2	20-- Dec.	31	Interest Receivable			275 00		2
3			Interest Income				275 00	3
4		31	Uncollectible Accounts Expense			7350 00		4
5			Allowance for Uncollectible Accounts				7350 00	5
6		31	Merchandise Inventory			25800 00		6
7			Income Summary				25800 00	7
8		31	Supplies Expense			2300 00		8
9			Supplies				2300 00	9
10		31	Insurance Expense			6000 00		10
11			Prepaid Insurance				6000 00	11
12		31	Depreciation Expense—Office Equipment			2800 00		12
13			Accumulated Depreciation—Office Equipment				2800 00	13
14		31	Depreciation Expense—Store Equipment			1700 60		14
15			Accumulated Depreciation—Store Equipment				1700 60	15
16		31	Interest Expense			555 16		16
17			Interest Payable				555 16	17
18		31	Federal Income Tax Expense			1752 70		18
19			Federal Income Tax Payable				1752 70	19
20								20
21								21
22								22
23								23
24								24
25								25
26								26
27								27
28								28
29								29
30								30
31								31
32								32

Name ______________________ Date ______________ Class ______________

22-4 WORK TOGETHER (continued)

2.

GENERAL JOURNAL PAGE 16

DATE		ACCOUNT TITLE	DOC. NO.	POST. REF.	DEBIT	CREDIT
		Closing Entries				
20-- Dec.	31	Sales			1,075,868.30	
		Purchases Discount			5,483.60	
		Purchases Returns and Allowances			2,716.14	
		Gain on Plant Assets			110.00	
		Interest Income			1,169.48	
		Income Summary				1,085,347.52
	31	Income Summary			1,035,721.69	
		Sales Discount				2,020.80
		Sales Returns and Allowances				8,347.20
		Purchases				737,464.80
		Advertising Expense				15,947.00
		Cash Short and Over				9.15
		Credit Card Fee Expense				10,066.94
		Depreciation Expense—Office Equipment				2,800.00
		Depreciation Expense—Store Equipment				1,700.60
		Insurance Expense				6,000.00
		Miscellaneous Expense				8,682.20
		Payroll Taxes Expense				14,966.00
		Rent Expense				28,915.00
		Repair Expense				3,485.00
		Salary Expense				158,964.00
		Supplies Expense				2,300.00
		Uncollectible Accounts Expense				7,350.00
		Utilities Expense				2,661.00
		Interest Expense				2,741.30
		Loss on Plant Assets				248.00
		Federal Income Tax Expense				21,052.70
	31	Income Summary			75,425.83	
		Retained Earnings				75,425.83
	31	Retained Earnings			43,200.00	
		Dividends				43,200.00

22-4 WORK TOGETHER (concluded)

3.

GENERAL JOURNAL PAGE 17

DATE		ACCOUNT TITLE	DOC. NO.	POST. REF.	DEBIT	CREDIT
		Reversing Entries				
20-- *Jan.*	*1*	*Interest Income*			*275 00*	
		Interest Receivable				*275 00*
	1	*Interest Payable*			*555 16*	
		Interest Expense				*555 16*
	1	*Federal Income Tax Payable*			*1752 70*	
		Federal Income Tax Expense				*1752 70*

Name ______________________ Date ____________ Class ____________

22-4 ON YOUR OWN, p. 660

Journalizing adjusting, closing, and reversing entries for a corporation

1.

GENERAL JOURNAL PAGE 18

DATE		ACCOUNT TITLE	DOC. NO.	POST. REF.	DEBIT	CREDIT
		Adjusting Entries				
20-- Dec.	31	*Interest Receivable*			160 00	
		Interest Income				160 00
	31	*Uncollectible Accounts Expense*			7312 00	
		Allowance for Uncollectible Accounts				7312 00
	31	*Merchandise Inventory*			2108 01	
		Income Summary				2108 01
	31	*Supplies Expense*			8415 75	
		Supplies				8415 75
	31	*Insurance Expense*			14600 00	
		Prepaid Insurance				14600 00
	31	*Depreciation Expense—Office Equipment*			6440 00	
		Accumulated Depreciation—Office Equipment				6440 00
	31	*Depreciation Expense—Store Equipment*			8250 00	
		Accumulated Depreciation—Store Equipment				8250 00
	31	*Interest Expense*			300 00	
		Interest Payable				300 00
	31	*Federal Income Tax Expense*			5296 94	
		Federal Income Tax Payable				5296 94

22-4 ON YOUR OWN (continued)

2.

GENERAL JOURNAL — PAGE 19

	DATE		ACCOUNT TITLE	DOC. NO.	POST. REF.	DEBIT	CREDIT
1			*Closing Entries*				
2	20-- Dec.	31	Sales			2,584,483.25	
3			Purchases Discount			7,891.17	
4			Purchases Returns and Allowances			6,148.20	
5			Gain on Plant Assets			2,458.00	
6			Interest Income			785.00	
7			Income Summary				2,601,765.62
8		31	Income Summary			2,433,768.15	
9			Sales Discount				12,485.28
10			Sales Returns and Allowances				22,894.10
11			Purchases				1,638,817.14
12			Advertising Expense				38,114.20
13			Cash Short and Over				15.33
14			Credit Card Fee Expense				18,122.10
15			Depreciation Expense—Office Equipment				6,440.00
16			Depreciation Expense—Store Equipment				8,250.00
17			Insurance Expense				14,600.00
18			Miscellaneous Expense				29,485.25
19			Payroll Taxes Expense				32,148.24
20			Rent Expense				54,000.00
21			Repair Expense				12,487.93
22			Salary Expense				421,584.99
23			Supplies Expense				8,415.75
24			Uncollectible Accounts Expense				7,312.00
25			Utilities Expense				23,199.90
26			Interest Expense				2,080.00
27			Loss on Plant Assets				2,019.00
28			Federal Income Tax Expense				81,296.94
29		31	Income Summary			170,105.48	
30			Retained Earnings				170,105.48
31		31	Retained Earnings			20,000.00	
32			Dividends				20,000.00
33							

Name ______________________ Date ______________ Class ______________

22-4 ON YOUR OWN (concluded)

3.

GENERAL JOURNAL PAGE 20

	DATE		ACCOUNT TITLE	DOC. NO.	POST. REF.	DEBIT	CREDIT	
1			*Reversing Entries*					1
2	20-- Jan.	1	Interest Income			160 00		2
3			Interest Receivable				160 00	3
4			Interest Payable			300 00		4
5			Interest Expense				300 00	5
6			Federal Income Tax Payable			5,296 94		6
7			Federal Income Tax Expense				5,296 94	7
8								8
9								9
10								10
11								11
12								12
13								13
14								14
15								15
16								16
17								17
18								18
19								19
20								20
21								21
22								22
23								23
24								24
25								25
26								26
27								27
28								28
29								29
30								30
31								31
32								32
33								33

22-1 APPLICATION PROBLEM, p. 662

Preparing a work sheet for a corporation

1., 2.

Donovan Lumber Corporation

Work Sheet

For Year Ended December 31, 20 – –

	Account Title	1 Trial Balance Debit	2 Trial Balance Credit	3 Adjustments Debit	4 Adjustments Credit	5 Income Statement Debit	6 Income Statement Credit	7 Balance Sheet Debit	8 Balance Sheet Credit	
1	Cash	3,848.58						3,848.58		1
2	Petty Cash	300.00						300.00		2
3	Notes Receivable	5,848.80						5,848.80		3
4	Interest Receivable			(a) 315.00				315.00		4
5	Accounts Receivable	57,187.80						57,187.80		5
6	Allowance for Uncoll. Accts.		66.48		(b) 6,850.00				6,916.48	6
7	Merchandise Inventory	78,858.00		(c) 2,426.50				81,284.50		7
8	Supplies	4,987.70			(d) 3,140.20			1,847.50		8
9	Prepaid Insurance	8,948.00			(e) 4,768.00			4,180.00		9
10	Office Equipment	26,488.00						26,488.00		10
11	Accum. Depr.—Office Equip.		8,488.00		(f) 3,128.00				11,616.00	11
12	Store Equipment	17,498.00						17,498.00		12
13	Accum. Depr.—Store Equip.		4,871.40		(g) 3,389.00				8,260.40	13
14	Notes Payable		30,000.00						30,000.00	14
15	Interest Payable				(h) 300.00				300.00	15
16	Accounts Payable		8,372.80						8,372.80	16
17	Employee Inc. Tax Payable		1,486.30						1,486.30	17
18	Federal Inc. Tax Payable				(i) 1,278.49				1,278.49	18
19	Social Security Tax Payable		1,209.81						1,209.81	19
20	Medicare Tax Payable		279.19						279.19	20
21	Sales Tax Payable		2,847.00						2,847.00	21
22	Unemploy. Tax Pay.—Fed.		29.25						29.25	22
23	Unemploy. Tax Pay.—State		195.00						195.00	23
24	Health Ins. Premiums Pay.		348.80						348.80	24
25	Dividends Payable		5,000.00						5,000.00	25
26	Capital Stock		50,000.00						50,000.00	26
27	Retained Earnings		30,823.18						30,823.18	27
28	Dividends	20,000.00						20,000.00		28
29	Income Summary				(c) 2,426.50		2,426.50			29
30	Sales		983,837.20				983,837.20			30
31	Sales Discount	1,894.50				1,894.50				31
32	Sales Ret. and Allowances	4,583.50				4,583.50				32

2. Total of Income Statement Credit column — $993,584.67

Less total of Income Statement Debit column before federal income tax — −920,470.70

Equals Net Income before Federal Income Tax — $ 73,113.97

Name _______________ Date _______________ Class _______________

22-1 APPLICATION PROBLEM (concluded)

Donovan Lumber Corporation

Work Sheet (continued)

For Year Ended December 31, 20 – –

ACCOUNT TITLE	1 TRIAL BALANCE DEBIT	2 TRIAL BALANCE CREDIT	3 ADJUSTMENTS DEBIT	4 ADJUSTMENTS CREDIT	5 INCOME STATEMENT DEBIT	6 INCOME STATEMENT CREDIT	7 BALANCE SHEET DEBIT	8 BALANCE SHEET CREDIT
Purchases	697318 50				*697318 50*			
Purchases Discount		4215 50				*4215 50*		
Purchases Ret. and Allow.		1848 47				*1848 47*		
Advertising Expense	9483 80				*9483 80*			
Cash Short and Over	10 20				*10 20*			
Credit Card Fee Expense	8482 90				*8482 90*			
Depr. Exp.—Office Equip.			(f) *3128 00*		*3128 00*			
Depr. Exp.—Store Equip.			(g) *3389 00*		*3389 00*			
Insurance Expense			(e) *4768 00*		*4768 00*			
Miscellaneous Expense	9184 80				*9184 80*			
Payroll Taxes Expense	12848 00				*12848 00*			
Rent Expense	15000 00				*15000 00*			
Repair Expense	4104 80				*4104 80*			
Salary Expense	125483 20				*125483 20*			
Supplies Expense			(d) *3140 20*		*3140 20*			
Uncollectible Accounts Exp.			(b) *6850 00*		*6850 00*			
Utilities Expense	7158 90				*7158 90*			
Gain on Plant Assets		715 00				*715 00*		
Interest Income		227 00		(a) *315 00*		*542 00*		
Interest Expense	3158 40		(h) *300 00*		*3458 40*			
Loss on Plant Assets	184 00				*184 00*			
Federal Income Tax Expense	12000 00		(i) *1278 49*		*13278 49*			
	1134860 38	1134860 38	*25595 19*	*25595 19*	*933749 19*	*993584 67*	*218798 18*	*158962 70*
Net Inc. after Fed. Inc. Tax					*59835 48*			*59835 48*
					993584 67	*993584 67*	*218798 18*	*218798 18*

2.

Net Income before Taxes	×	Tax Rate	=	Federal Income Tax Amount
$50,000.00	×	15%	=	*$ 7,500.00*
Plus *23,113.97*	×	25%	=	*5,778.49*
Plus	×	34%	=	
Plus	×	39%	=	
Total *$73,113.97*				*$13,278.49*

22-2 APPLICATION PROBLEM, p. 662

Preparing an income statement for a corporation

1., 2.

Donovan Lumber Corporation
Income Statement
For Year Ended December 31, 20 – –

					% OF NET SALES
Operating Revenue:					
Sales			983,837.20		
Less: Sales Discount		1,894.50			
Sales Returns and Allowances		4,583.50	6,478.00		
Net Sales				977,359.20	100.0
Cost of Merchandise Sold:					
Merchandise Inventory, Jan. 1, 20 – –			78,858.00		
Purchases		697,318.50			
Less: Purchases Discount	4,215.50				
Purchases Ret. and Allow.	1,848.47	6,063.97			
Net Purchases			691,254.53		
Total Cost of Mdse. Avail. for Sale			770,112.53		
Less Mdse. Inventory, Dec. 31, 20 – –			81,284.50		
Cost of Merchandise Sold				688,828.03	70.5
Gross Profit on Operations				288,531.17	29.5
Operating Expenses:					
Advertising Expense			9,483.80		
Cash Short and Over			10.20		
Credit Card Fee Expense			8,482.90		
Depr. Expense—Office Equipment			3,128.00		
Depr. Expense—Store Equipment			3,389.00		
Insurance Expense			4,768.00		
Miscellaneous Expense			9,184.80		
Payroll Taxes Expense			12,848.00		
Rent Expense			15,000.00		
Repair Expense			4,104.80		
Salary Expense			125,483.20		
Supplies Expense			3,140.20		
Uncollectible Accounts Expense			6,850.00		
Utilities Expense			7,158.90		
Total Operating Expenses				213,031.80	21.8
Income from Operations				75,499.37	7.7

Name ____________________ Date ____________ Class ____________

22-2 APPLICATION PROBLEM (concluded)

1., 2.

Donovan Lumber Corporation

Income Statement (continued)

For Year Ended December 31, 20 – –

					% OF NET SALES
Other Revenue:					
Gain on Plant Assets		715 00			
Interest Income		542 00			
Total Other Revenue			1,257 00		
Other Expenses:					
Interest Expense		3,458 40			
Loss on Plant Assets		184 00			
Total Other Expenses			3,642 40		
Net Deduction				2,385 40	*0.2*
Net Income before Fed. Inc. Tax				73,113 97	*7.5*
Less Federal Income Tax Expense				13,278 49	
Net Income after Federal Income Tax				59,835 48	

3.

	Acceptable %	Actual %	Positive Result Yes	Positive Result No	Recommended Action If Needed
Cost of merchandise sold	Not more than 70.0%	*70.5%*		✓	*Identify ways of reducing the cost of merchandise or increase the unit sales price of merchandise.*
Gross profit on operations	Not less than 30.0%	*29.5%*		✓	*Changes in purchasing or pricing policies will increase this percentage.*
Total operating expenses	Not more than 25.0%	*21.8%*	✓		*None*
Income from operations	Not less than 5.0%	*7.7%*	✓		*None*
Net deduction from other revenue and expenses	Not more than 0.1%	*0.2%*		✓	*Review interest expense transactions and pursue ways of reducing the cost of long-term borrowing.*
Net income before federal income tax	Not less than 4.9%	*7.5%*	✓		*None*

22-3 APPLICATION PROBLEM, p. 663

Preparing a statement of stockholders' equity and balance sheet for a corporation

1.

Donovan Lumber Corporation

Statement of Stockholders' Equity

For Year Ended December 31, 20 – –

Capital Stock:			
$5.00 Par Value			
January 1, 20 – –, 8,000 Shares Issued		40 000 00	
Issued during Current Year, 2,000 Shares		10 000 00	
Balance, December 31, 20 – –, 10,000 Shares Issued			50 000 00
Retained Earnings:			
Balance, January 1, 20 – –		30 823 18	
Net Income after Federal Income Tax for 20 – –	59 835 48		
Less Dividends Declared during 20 – –	20 000 00		
Net Increase during 20 – –		39 835 48	
Balance, December 31, 20 – –			70 658 66
Total Stockholders' Equity, December 31, 20 – –			120 658 66

Name ________________ Date ________ Class ________

22-3 APPLICATION PROBLEM (continued)

2.

Donovan Lumber Corporation

Balance Sheet

December 31, 20 – –

Assets			
Current Assets:			
Cash		3,848.58	
Petty Cash		300.00	
Notes Receivable		5,848.80	
Interest Receivable		315.00	
Accounts Receivable	57,187.80		
Less Allowance for Uncollectible Accounts	6,916.48	50,271.32	
Merchandise Inventory		81,284.50	
Supplies		1,847.50	
Prepaid Insurance		4,180.00	
Total Current Assets			147,895.70
Plant Assets:			
Office Equipment	26,488.00		
Less Accumulated Depreciation—Office Equipment	11,616.00	14,872.00	
Store Equipment	17,498.00		
Less Accumulated Depreciation—Store Equipment	8,260.40	9,237.60	
Total Plant Assets			24,109.60
Total Assets			172,005.30
Liabilities			
Current Liabilities:			
Notes Payable		30,000.00	
Interest Payable		300.00	
Accounts Payable		8,372.80	
Employee Income Tax Payable		1,486.30	
Federal Income Tax Payable		1,278.49	
Social Security Tax Payable		1,209.81	
Medicare Tax Payable		279.19	
Sales Tax Payable		2,847.00	
Unemployment Tax Payable—Federal		29.25	
Unemployment Tax Payable—State		195.00	
Health Insurance Premiums Payable		348.80	
Dividends Payable		5,000.00	
Total Liabilities			51,346.64

22-3 APPLICATION PROBLEM (concluded)

2.

Donovan Lumber Corporation

Balance Sheet (continued)

December 31, 20 – –

Stockholders' Equity			
Capital Stock		50 000 00	
Retained Earnings		70 658 66	
Total Stockholders' Equity			120 658 66
Total Liabilities and Stockholders' Equity			172 005 30

3., 4.

	Acceptable	Actual	Positive Result: Yes	Positive Result: No	Recommended Action If Needed
Working capital	Not less than $100,000	*$96,549.06*		✓	*Consider obtaining long-term financing to reduce current liabilities.*
Current ratio	Between 3.0 to 1 and 3.5 to 1	*2.88 to 1*		✓	*Same as above.*

Name ______________________ Date ______________ Class ______________

22-4 APPLICATION PROBLEM, p. 663

Journalizing adjusting, closing, and reversing entries for a corporation

1.

GENERAL JOURNAL PAGE 15

	DATE		ACCOUNT TITLE	DOC. NO.	POST. REF.	DEBIT	CREDIT	
1			*Adjusting Entries*					1
2	20-- Dec.	31	Interest Receivable			315 00		2
3			Interest Income				315 00	3
4		31	Uncollectible Accounts Expense			6850 00		4
5			Allowance for Uncollectible Accounts				6850 00	5
6		31	Merchandise Inventory			2426 50		6
7			Income Summary				2426 50	7
8		31	Supplies Expense			3140 20		8
9			Supplies				3140 20	9
10		31	Insurance Expense			4768 00		10
11			Prepaid Insurance				4768 00	11
12		31	Depreciation Expense—Office Equipment			3128 00		12
13			Accumulated Depreciation—Office Equipment				3128 00	13
14		31	Depreciation Expense—Store Equipment			3389 00		14
15			Accumulated Depreciation—Store Equipment				3389 00	15
16		31	Interest Expense			300 00		16
17			Interest Payable				300 00	17
18		31	Federal Income Tax Expense			1278 49		18
19			Federal Income Tax Payable				1278 49	19
20								20
21								21
22								22
23								23
24								24
25								25
26								26
27								27
28								28
29								29
30								30
31								31
32								32

22-4 APPLICATION PROBLEM (continued)

2.

GENERAL JOURNAL — PAGE 16

DATE		ACCOUNT TITLE	DOC. NO.	POST. REF.	DEBIT	CREDIT
		Closing Entries				
20-- Dec.	31	Sales			983,837.20	
		Purchases Discount			4,215.50	
		Purchases Returns and Allowances			1,848.47	
		Gain on Plant Assets			715.00	
		Interest Income			542.00	
		Income Summary				991,158.17
	31	Income Summary			933,749.19	
		Sales Discount				1,894.50
		Sales Returns and Allowances				4,583.50
		Purchases				697,318.50
		Advertising Expense				9,483.80
		Cash Short and Over				10.20
		Credit Card Fee Expense				8,482.90
		Depreciation Expense—Office Equipment				3,128.00
		Depreciation Expense—Store Equipment				3,389.00
		Insurance Expense				4,768.00
		Miscellaneous Expense				9,184.80
		Payroll Taxes Expense				12,848.00
		Rent Expense				15,000.00
		Repair Expense				4,104.80
		Salary Expense				125,483.20
		Supplies Expense				3,140.20
		Uncollectible Accounts Expense				6,850.00
		Utilities Expense				7,158.90
		Interest Expense				3,458.40
		Loss on Plant Assets				184.00
		Federal Income Tax Expense				13,278.49
	31	Income Summary			59,835.48	
		Retained Earnings				59,835.48
	31	Retained Earnings			20,000.00	
		Dividends				20,000.00

Name ______________________ Date ____________ Class ____________

22-4 APPLICATION PROBLEM (concluded)

3.

GENERAL JOURNAL PAGE 17

	DATE		ACCOUNT TITLE	DOC. NO.	POST. REF.	DEBIT	CREDIT	
1			*Reversing Entries*					1
2	20-- *Jan.*	*1*	*Interest Income*			*315 00*		2
3			*Interest Receivable*				*315 00*	3
4		*1*	*Interest Payable*			*300 00*		4
5			*Interest Expense*				*300 00*	5
6		*1*	*Federal Income Tax Payable*			*1278 49*		6
7			*Federal Income Tax Expense*				*1278 49*	7
8								8
9								9
10								10
11								11
12								12
13								13
14								14
15								15
16								16
17								17
18								18
19								19
20								20
21								21
22								22
23								23
24								24
25								25
26								26
27								27
28								28
29								29
30								30
31								31
32								32
33								33

22-5 MASTERY PROBLEM, pp. 663, 664

Preparing a work sheet, financial statement, and end-of-fiscal-period entries for a corporation

1.

Benford Corporation
Work Sheet
For Year Ended December 31, 20 – –

	ACCOUNT TITLE	1 TRIAL BALANCE DEBIT	2 TRIAL BALANCE CREDIT	3 ADJUSTMENTS DEBIT	4 ADJUSTMENTS CREDIT	5 INCOME STATEMENT DEBIT	6 INCOME STATEMENT CREDIT	7 BALANCE SHEET DEBIT	8 BALANCE SHEET CREDIT	
1	Cash	2,518.25						2,518.25		1
2	Petty Cash	500.00						500.00		2
3	Notes Receivable	4,000.00						4,000.00		3
4	Interest Receivable			(a) 80.00				80.00		4
5	Accounts Receivable	125,848.25						125,848.25		5
6	Allowance for Uncoll. Accts.	160.00			(b) 5,670.00				5,510.00	6
7	Merchandise Inventory	288,318.08			(c) 5,290.00			283,028.08		7
8	Supplies	6,481.28			(d) 5,482.29			998.99		8
9	Prepaid Insurance	14,000.00			(e) 12,000.00			2,000.00		9
10	Office Equipment	29,148.22						29,148.22		10
11	Accum. Depr.—Office Equip.		8,710.00		(f) 5,480.00				14,190.00	11
12	Store Equipment	27,158.00						27,158.00		12
13	Accum. Depr.—Store Equip.		18,160.00		(g) 5,060.00				23,220.00	13
14	Notes Payable		25,000.00						25,000.00	14
15	Interest Payable				(h) 312.50				312.50	15
16	Accounts Payable		32,158.29						32,158.29	16
17	Employee Inc. Tax Payable		2,458.80						2,458.80	17
18	Federal Inc. Tax Payable				(i) 3,522.81				3,522.81	18
19	Social Security Tax Payable		2,121.31						2,121.31	19
20	Medicare Tax Payable		512.69						512.69	20
21	Sales Tax Payable		2,518.66						2,518.66	21
22	Unemploy. Tax Pay.—Fed.		45.60						45.60	22
23	Unemploy. Tax Pay.—State		292.80						292.80	23
24	Health Ins. Premiums Pay.		672.00						672.00	24
25	Dividends Payable		8,000.00						8,000.00	25
26	Capital Stock		150,000.00						150,000.00	26
27	Retained Earnings		149,183.00						149,183.00	27
28	Dividends	32,000.00						32,000.00		28
29	Income Summary			(c) 5,290.00		5,290.00				29
30	Sales		2251,893.17				2251,893.17			30
31	Sales Discount	5,894.36				5,894.36				31
32	Sales Ret. and Allowances	15,487.39				15,487.39				32

Total of Income Statement Credit column	$2,273,471.35
Less total of Income Statement Debit column before federal income tax	−2,157,387.21
Equals Net Income before Federal Income Tax	$ 116,084.14

22-5 MASTERY PROBLEM (continued)

Benford Corporation

Work Sheet (continued)

For Year Ended December 31, 20 – –

	Account Title	1 Trial Balance Debit	2 Trial Balance Credit	3 Adjustments Debit	4 Adjustments Credit	5 Income Statement Debit	6 Income Statement Credit	7 Balance Sheet Debit	8 Balance Sheet Credit	
33	Purchases	1498 183 08				1498 183 08				33
34	Purchases Discount		13 118 02				13 118 02			34
35	Purchases Ret. and Allow.		6 184 16				6 184 16			35
36	Advertising Expense	16 486 90				16 486 90				36
37	Cash Short and Over	16 88				16 88				37
38	Credit Card Fee Expense	8 489 33				8 489 33				38
39	Depr. Exp.—Office Equip.			(f) 5 480 00		5 480 00				39
40	Depr. Exp.—Store Equip.			(g) 5 060 00		5 060 00				40
41	Insurance Expense			(e) 12 000 00		12 000 00				41
42	Miscellaneous Expense	42 186 30				42 186 30				42
43	Payroll Taxes Expense	32 184 02				32 184 02				43
44	Rent Expense	45 000 00				45 000 00				44
45	Repair Expense	6 154 99				6 154 99				45
46	Salary Expense	421 548 36				421 548 36				46
47	Supplies Expense			(d) 5 482 29		5 482 29				47
48	Uncollectible Accounts Exp.			(b) 5 670 00		5 670 00				48
49	Utilities Expense	20 445 61				20 445 61				49
50	Gain on Plant Assets		1 548 00				1 548 00			50
51	Interest Income		648 00		(a) 80 00		728 00			51
52	Interest Expense	3 600 00		(h) 312 50		3 912 50				52
53	Loss on Plant Assets	2 415 20				2 415 20				53
54	Federal Income Tax Expense	25 000 00		(i) 3 522 81		28 522 81				54
55		2673 224 50	2673 224 50	42 897 60	42 897 60	2185 910 02	2273 471 35	507 279 79	419 718 46	55
56	Net Inc. after Fed. Inc. Tax					87 561 33			87 561 33	56
57						2273 471 35	2273 471 35	507 279 79	507 279 79	57

	Net Income before Taxes	×	Tax Rate	=	Federal Income Tax Amount
	$ 50,000.00	×	15%	=	*$ 7,500.00*
Plus	25,000.00	×	25%	=	*6,250.00*
Plus	25,000.00	×	34%	=	*8,500.00*
Plus	*16,084.14*	×	39%	=	*6,272.81*
Total	*$116,084.14*				*$28,522.81*

22-5 MASTERY PROBLEM (continued)

2.

Benford Corporation
Income Statement
For Year Ended December 31, 20 – –

					% OF NET SALES
Operating Revenue:					
Sales			2,251,893.17		
Less: Sales Discount		5,894.36			
Sales Returns and Allowances		15,487.39	21,381.75		
Net Sales				2,230,511.42	100.0
Cost of Merchandise Sold:					
Merchandise Inventory, Jan. 1, 20 – –			288,318.08		
Purchases		1,498,183.08			
Less: Purchases Discount	13,118.02				
Purchases Ret. and Allow.	6,184.16	19,302.18			
Net Purchases			1,478,880.90		
Total Cost of Mdse. Avail. for Sale			1,767,198.98		
Less Mdse. Inventory, Dec. 31, 20 – –			283,028.08		
Cost of Merchandise Sold				1,484,170.90	66.5
Gross Profit on Operations				746,340.52	33.5
Operating Expenses:					
Advertising Expense			16,486.90		
Cash Short and Over			16.88		
Credit Card Fee Expense			8,489.33		
Depr. Expense—Office Equipment			5,480.00		
Depr. Expense—Store Equipment			5,060.00		
Insurance Expense			12,000.00		
Miscellaneous Expense			42,186.30		
Payroll Taxes Expense			32,184.02		
Rent Expense			45,000.00		
Repair Expense			6,154.99		
Salary Expense			421,548.36		
Supplies Expense			5,482.29		
Uncollectible Accounts Expense			5,670.00		
Utilities Expense			20,445.61		
Total Operating Expenses				626,204.68	28.1
Income from Operations				120,135.84	5.4
Other Revenue:					
Gain on Plant Assets		1,548.00			
Interest Income		728.00			
Total Other Income			2,276.00		
Other Expenses:					
Interest Expense		3,912.50			
Loss on Plant Assets		2,415.20			
Total Other Expenses			6,327.70		
Net Deduction				4,051.70	0.2
Net Income before Federal Income Tax				116,084.14	5.2
Less Federal Income Tax Expense				28,522.81	
Net Income after Federal Income Tax				87,561.33	

Name ______________________ Date __________ Class __________

22-5 MASTERY PROBLEM (continued)

3. Income Statement Analysis

	Acceptable %	Actual %	Positive Result Yes	Positive Result No	Recommended Action If Needed
Cost of merchandise sold	Not more than 70.0%	*66.5%*	✓		*None*
Gross profit on operations	Not less than 30.0%	*33.5%*	✓		*None*
Total operating expenses	Not more than 25.0%	*28.1%*		✓	*Review and identify excessive expenses so they may be controlled.*
Income from operations	Not less than 5.0%	*5.4%*	✓		*None*
Net deduction from other revenue and expenses	Not more than 0.1%	*0.2%*		✓	*Control costs to minimize having notes payable and the related interest expense.*
Net income before federal income tax	Not less than 4.9%	*5.2%*	✓		*Controlling expenses will further improve this percentage.*

4.

Benford Corporation

Statement of Stockholders' Equity

For Year Ended December 31, 20 – –

Captial Stock:			
$10.00 Per Share			
January 1, 20 – –, 14,000 Shares Issued		*140 0 0 0 00*	
Issued during Current Year, 1,000 shares		*10 0 0 0 00*	
Balance, December 31, 20 – –, 15,000 Shares Issued			*150 0 0 0 00*
Retained Earnings:			
Balance, January 1, 20 – –		*149 1 8 3 00*	
Net Income after Federal Income Tax for 20 – –	*87 5 6 1 33*		
Less Dividends Declared during 20 – –	*32 0 0 0 00*		
Net Increase during 20 – –		*55 5 6 1 33*	
Balance, December 31, 20 – –			*204 7 4 4 33*
Total Stockholders' Equity, December 31, 20 – –			*354 7 4 4 33*

5.

Benford Corporation

Balance Sheet

December 31, 20 – –

Assets			
Current Assets:			
Cash		2,518.25	
Petty Cash		500.00	
Notes Receivable		4,000.00	
Interest Receivable		80.00	
Accounts Receivable	125,848.25		
Less Allowance for Uncollectible Accounts	5,510.00	120,338.25	
Merchandise Inventory		283,028.08	
Supplies		998.99	
Prepaid Insurance		2,000.00	
Total Current Assets			413,463.57
Plant Assets:			
Office Equipment	29,148.22		
Less Accumulated Depreciation—Office Equipment	14,190.00	14,958.22	
Store Equipment	27,158.00		
Less Accumulated Depreciation—Store Equipment	23,220.00	3,938.00	
Total Plant Assets			18,896.22
Total Assets			432,359.79
Liabilities			
Current Liabilities:			
Notes Payable		25,000.00	
Interest Payable		312.50	
Accounts Payable		32,158.29	
Employee Income Tax Payable		2,458.80	
Federal Income Tax Payable		3,522.81	
Social Security Tax Payable		2,121.31	
Medicare Tax Payable		512.69	
Sales Tax Payable		2,518.66	
Unemployment Tax Payable—Federal		45.60	
Unemployment Tax Payable—State		292.80	
Health Insurance Premiums Payable		672.00	
Dividends Payable		8,000.00	
Total Liabilities			77,615.46
Stockholders' Equity			
Capital Stock		150,000.00	
Retained Earnings		204,744.33	
Total Stockholders' Equity			354,744.33
Total Liabilities and Stockholders' Equity			432,359.79

Name ______________________ Date ____________ Class ____________

22-5 MASTERY PROBLEM (continued)

6. Balance Sheet Analysis

	Acceptable	Actual	Positive Result		Recommended Action If Needed
			Yes	No	
Working capital	Not less than $150,000	*$335,848.11*	✓		*None*
Current ratio	Between 3.0 to 1 and 4.0 to 1	*5.3 to 1*		✓	*Company appears to have too many current assets. Evaluate current assets for excessive amounts. Accounts receivable collections could be accelerated, inventory levels could be reduced.*

7.

GENERAL JOURNAL PAGE 15

	DATE		ACCOUNT TITLE	DOC. NO.	POST. REF.	DEBIT	CREDIT	
1			*Adjusting Entries*					1
2	20-- *Dec.*	*31*	*Interest Receivable*			*80 00*		2
3			*Interest Income*				*80 00*	3
4		*31*	*Uncollectible Accounts Expense*			*5,670 00*		4
5			*Allowance for Uncollectible Accounts*				*5,670 00*	5
6		*31*	*Income Summary*			*5,290 00*		6
7			*Merchandise Inventory*				*5,290 00*	7
8		*31*	*Supplies Expense*			*5,482 29*		8
9			*Supplies*				*5,482 29*	9
10		*31*	*Insurance Expense*			*12,000 00*		10
11			*Prepaid Insurance*				*12,000 00*	11
12		*31*	*Depreciation Expense—Office Equipment*			*5,480 00*		12
13			*Accumulated Depreciation—Office Equipment*				*5,480 00*	13
14		*31*	*Depreciation Expense—Store Equipment*			*5,060 00*		14
15			*Accumulated Depreciation—Store Equipment*				*5,060 00*	15
16		*31*	*Interest Expense*			*312 50*		16
17			*Interest Payable*				*312 50*	17
18		*31*	*Federal Income Tax Expense*			*3,522 81*		18
19			*Federal Income Tax Payable*				*3,522 81*	19
20								20
21								21

22-5 MASTERY PROBLEM (continued)

8.

GENERAL JOURNAL PAGE 16

	DATE		ACCOUNT TITLE	DOC. NO.	POST. REF.	DEBIT	CREDIT	
1			*Closing Entries*					1
2	20-- *Dec.*	*31*	*Sales*			*2251893 17*		2
3			*Purchases Discount*			*13118 02*		3
4			*Purchases Returns and Allowances*			*6184 16*		4
5			*Gain on Plant Assets*			*1548 00*		5
6			*Interest Income*			*728 00*		6
7			*Income Summary*				*2273471 35*	7
8		*31*	*Income Summary*			*2180620 02*		8
9			*Sales Discount*				*5894 36*	9
10			*Sales Returns and Allowances*				*15487 39*	10
11			*Purchases*				*1498183 08*	11
12			*Advertising Expense*				*16486 90*	12
13			*Cash Short and Over*				*16 88*	13
14			*Credit Card Fee Expense*				*8489 33*	14
15			*Depreciation Expense—Office Equipment*				*5480 00*	15
16			*Depreciation Expense—Store Equipment*				*5060 00*	16
17			*Insurance Expense*				*12000 00*	17
18			*Miscellaneous Expense*				*42186 30*	18
19			*Payroll Taxes Expense*				*32184 02*	19
20			*Rent Expense*				*45000 00*	20
21			*Repair Expense*				*6154 99*	21
22			*Salary Expense*				*421548 36*	22
23			*Supplies Expense*				*5482 29*	23
24			*Uncollectible Accounts Expense*				*5670 00*	24
25			*Utilities Expense*				*20445 61*	25
26			*Interest Expense*				*3912 50*	26
27			*Loss on Plant Assets*				*2415 20*	27
28			*Federal Income Tax Expense*				*28522 81*	28
29		*31*	*Income Summary*			*87561 33*		29
30			*Retained Earnings*				*87561 33*	30
31		*31*	*Retained Earnings*			*32000 00*		31
32			*Dividends*				*32000 00*	32
33								33

Name ______________________ Date ____________ Class ____________

22-5 MASTERY PROBLEM (concluded)

9.

GENERAL JOURNAL PAGE 17

	DATE		ACCOUNT TITLE	DOC. NO.	POST. REF.	DEBIT	CREDIT	
1			*Reversing Entries*					1
2	20-- *Jan.*	*1*	*Interest Income*			*80 00*		2
3			*Interest Receivable*				*80 00*	3
4		*1*	*Interest Payable*			*312 50*		4
5			*Interest Expense*				*312 50*	5
6		*1*	*Federal Income Tax Payable*			*3522 81*		6
7			*Federal Income Tax Expense*				*3522 81*	7

22-6 CHALLENGE PROBLEM, p. 664

Analyzing financial strength

1.

Name of Corporation	Working Capital	Current Ratio
1.		
2.		

Calculations:

2.

Working capital is a measure of the financial resources available for the daily operations of the business. Many people inside and outside of a corporation wish to be sure that the company has sufficient working capital to meet payrolls, satisfy accounts payable, pay off loans, and enjoy enough business success to be considered a good investment. Employees, creditors, and investors can evaluate the appropriateness of a company's working capital by comparing the company's amount of working capital to the amounts of working capital for other corporations in the same industry. A company with working capital higher than most other companies in the same industry might seem to be a strong company. In addition, people may be interested in the differences in financial strength between companies in different industries. For example, businesses in a service industry would have no merchandise inventory and might be expected to have low amounts of working capital. Businesses in a merchandise industry might be expected to have higher amounts of working capital. The same contrasts and comparisons apply to the current ratio.

22-6 CHALLENGE PROBLEM (concluded)

3.

A current ratio that is too high might indicate that the business has more capital invested in current assets than is needed to run the business. For example, a corporation may have excess merchandise inventory that has little likelihood of being sold.

REINFORCEMENT ACTIVITY 3 PART B, p. 668

An accounting cycle for a corporation: end-of-fiscal-period work

10., 11., 12.

Sparkle, Inc.

Work Sheet

For Year Ended December 31, 20X4

	Account Title	1 Trial Balance Debit	2 Trial Balance Credit	3 Adjustments Debit	4 Adjustments Credit	5 Income Statement Debit	6 Income Statement Credit	7 Balance Sheet Debit	8 Balance Sheet Credit	
1	Cash	8,100.70						8,100.70		1
2	Petty Cash	200.00						200.00		2
3	Notes Receivable	3,600.00						3,600.00		3
4	Interest Receivable			(a) 24.00				24.00		4
5	Accounts Receivable	7,894.60						7,894.60		5
6	Allowance for Uncoll. Accts.	1,469.40			(b) 3,600.00				2,130.60	6
7	Merchandise Inventory	74,176.95		(c) 6,315.00				80,491.95		7
8	Supplies	3,099.05			(d) 2,674.00			425.05		8
9	Prepaid Insurance	8,600.00			(e) 8,000.00			600.00		9
10	Office Equipment	23,830.00						23,830.00		10
11	Accum. Depr.—Office Equip.		7,160.00		(f) 6,520.00				13,680.00	11
12	Warehouse Equipment	26,110.00						26,110.00		12
13	Accum. Depr.—Warehouse Equip.		7,040.00		(g) 4,210.00				11,250.00	13
14	Notes Payable		16,000.00						16,000.00	14
15	Interest Payable				(h) 155.00				155.00	15
16	Accounts Payable		14,112.65						14,112.65	16
17	Federal Income Tax Pay.				(i) 2,103.16				2,103.16	17
18	Employee Income Tax Pay.		310.00						310.00	18
19	Social Security Tax Pay.		691.92						691.92	19
20	Medicare Tax Payable		161.82						161.82	20
21	Sales Tax Payable		6,210.66						6,210.66	21
22	Unemploy. Tax Pay.—Fed.		21.53						21.53	22
23	Unemploy. Tax Pay.—State		145.29						145.29	23
24	Health Ins. Premiums Pay.		1,105.00						1,105.00	24
25	Dividends Payable		5,000.00						5,000.00	25
26	Capital Stock		30,000.00						30,000.00	26
27	Retained Earnings		23,889.20						23,889.20	27
28	Dividends	20,000.00						20,000.00		28
29	Income Summary				(c) 6,315.00		6,315.00			29
30	Sales		779,210.90				779,210.90			30
31	Sales Discount	1,889.20				1,889.20				31

Name ____________ Date ____________ Class ____________

REINFORCEMENT ACTIVITY 3 PART B (continued)

Sparkle, Inc.

Work Sheet (continued)

For Year Ended December 31, 20X4

	ACCOUNT TITLE	1 TRIAL BALANCE DEBIT	2 TRIAL BALANCE CREDIT	3 ADJUSTMENTS DEBIT	4 ADJUSTMENTS CREDIT	5 INCOME STATEMENT DEBIT	6 INCOME STATEMENT CREDIT	7 BALANCE SHEET DEBIT	8 BALANCE SHEET CREDIT	
32	Sales Returns and Allow.	6,174.80				6,174.80				32
33	Purchases	529,022.40				529,022.40				33
34	Purchases Discount		3,596.08				3,596.08			34
35	Purchases Returns and Allow.		3,236.00				3,236.00			35
36	Advertising Expense	9,606.70				9,606.70				36
37	Cash Short and Over	20.09				20.09				37
38	Credit Card Fee Expense	14,529.40				14,529.40				38
39	Depr. Expense—Office Equip.	240.00		(f) 6,520.00		6,760.00				39
40	Depr. Expense—Ware. Equip.	440.00		(g) 4,210.00		4,650.00				40
41	Insurance Expense			(e) 8,000.00		8,000.00				41
42	Miscellaneous Expense	5,828.32				5,828.32				42
43	Payroll Taxes Expense	10,669.44				10,669.44				43
44	Rent Expense	21,000.00				21,000.00				44
45	Repairs Expense	1,394.80				1,394.80				45
46	Salary Expense	104,878.00				104,878.00				46
47	Supplies Expense			(d) 2,674.00		2,674.00				47
48	Uncollectible Accounts Exp.			(b) 3,600.00		3,600.00				48
49	Utilities Expense	7,236.20				7,236.20				49
50	Gain on Plant Assets		745.00				745.00			50
51	Interest Income		414.00		(a) 24.00		438.00			51
52	Interest Expense	2,750.00		(h) 155.00		2,905.00				52
53	Loss on Plant Assets	290.00				290.00				53
54	Federal Income Tax Expense	6,000.00		(i) 2,103.16		8,103.16				54
55		899,050.05	899,050.05	33,601.16	33,601.16	749,231.51	793,540.98	171,276.30	126,966.83	55
56	Net Income after Fed. In. Tax					44,309.47			44,309.47	56
57						793,540.98	793,540.98	171,276.30	171,276.30	57

Total of Income Statement Credit column	$793,540.98
Less total of Income Statement Debit column before federal income tax	−741,128.35
Equals Net Income before Federal Income Tax	$ 52,412.63

Net Income before Taxes	×	Tax Rate	=	Federal Income Tax Amount
$50,000.00	×	15%	=	$7,500.00
$2,412.63	×	25%	=	603.16
				$8,103.16

13.

Sparkle, Inc.

Income Statement

For Year Ended December 31, 20X4

					% OF NET SALES
Operating Revenue:					
Sales			779,210.90		
Less: Sales Discount		1,889.20			
Sales Returns and Allow.		6,174.80	8,064.00		
Net Sales				771,146.90	100.0
Cost of Merchandise Sold:					
Merchandise Inventory, Jan. 1, 20 – –			74,176.95		
Purchases		529,022.40			
Less: Purchases Discount	3,596.08				
Purchases Returns and Allow.	3,236.00	6,832.08			
Net Purchases			522,190.32		
Total Cost of Mdse. Avail. for Sale			596,367.27		
Less Mdse. Inventory, Dec. 31, 20 – –			80,491.95		
Cost of Merchandise Sold				515,875.32	66.9
Gross Profit on Operations				255,271.58	33.1
Operating Expenses:					
Advertising Expense			9,606.70		
Cash Short and Over			20.09		
Credit Card Fee Expense			14,529.40		
Depr. Expense—Office Equipment			6,760.00		
Depr. Expense—Warehouse Equipment			4,650.00		
Insurance Expense			8,000.00		
Miscellaneous Expense			5,828.32		
Payroll Taxes Expense			10,669.44		
Rent Expense			21,000.00		
Repairs Expense			1,394.80		
Salary Expense			104,878.00		
Supplies Expense			2,674.00		
Uncollectible Accounts Expense			3,600.00		
Utilities Expense			7,236.20		
Total Operating Expenses				200,846.95	26.0
Income from Operations				54,424.63	7.1
Other Revenue:					
Gain on Plant Assets		745.00			
Interest Income		438.00			
Total Other Income			1,183.00		
Other Expenses:					
Interest Expense		2,905.00			
Loss on Plant Assets		290.00			
Total Other Expenses			3,195.00		
Net Deduction				2,012.00	0.3
Net Income before Federal Income Tax				52,412.63	6.8
Less Federal Income Tax Expense				8,103.16	
Net Income after Federal Income Tax				44,309.47	

Name ______________________ Date ____________ Class ____________

REINFORCEMENT ACTIVITY 3 PART B (continued)

14.

	Acceptable %	Actual %	Positive Result		Recommended Action If Needed
			Yes	No	
Cost of merchandise sold	Not more than 62.0%	*66.9%*		✓	*Identify ways of reducing the cost of merchandise or increase the unit sales price of merchandise.*
Gross profit on operations	Not less than 38.0%	*33.1%*		✓	*Changes in purchasing or pricing policies will increase this percentage.*
Total operating expenses	Not more than 28.0%	*26.0%*	✓		*None*
Income from operations	Not less than 10.0%	*7.1%*		✓	*Changes in purchasing or pricing policies will increase this percentage.*
Net deductions from other revenue and expenses	Not more than 0.5%	*0.3%*	✓		*None*
Net income before federal income tax	Not less than 9.5%	*6.8%*		✓	*Changes in purchasing or pricing policies will increase this percentage.*

15.

Net Income after Federal Income Tax	÷	Number of Shares Outstanding	=	Earnings per Share
$44,309.47	÷	*3,000*	=	*$14.77*

Market Price per Share	÷	Earnings per Share	=	Price-Earnings Ratio
$225.00	÷	*$14.77*	=	*15.2*

16.

Sparkle, Inc.

Statement of Stockholders' Equity

For Year Ended December 31, 20X4

Capital Stock:			
$10.00 Per Share			
January 1, 20 – –, 3,000 Shares Issued		30 000 00	
Issued during Current Year, None		0 00	
Balance, December 31, 20 – –, 3,000 Shares Issued			30 000 00
Retained Earnings:			
Balance, January 1, 20 – –		23 889 20	
Net Income after Federal Income Tax for 20 – –	44 309 47		
Less Dividends Declared during 20 – –	20 000 00		
Net Increase during 20 – –		24 309 47	
Balance, December 31, 20 – –			48 198 67
Total Stockholders' Equity, December 31, 20 – –			78 198 67

Name ______________________ Date ______________ Class ______________

REINFORCEMENT ACTIVITY 3 PART B (continued)

17.

Sparkle, Inc.

Balance Sheet

December 31, 20X4

Assets			
Current Assets:			
Cash		8,100.70	
Petty Cash		200.00	
Notes Receivable		3,600.00	
Interest Receivable		24.00	
Accounts Receivable	7,894.60		
Less Allowance for Uncollectible Accounts	2,130.60	5,764.00	
Merchandise Inventory		80,491.95	
Supplies		425.05	
Prepaid Insurance		600.00	
Total Current Assets			99,205.70
Plant Assets:			
Office Equipment	23,830.00		
Less Accumulated Depreciation—Office Equipment	13,680.00	10,150.00	
Warehouse Equipment	26,110.00		
Less Accumulated Depreciation—Warehouse Equipment	11,250.00	14,860.00	
Total Plant Assets			25,010.00
Total Assets			124,215.70
Liabilities			
Current Liabilities:			
Notes Payable		16,000.00	
Interest Payable		155.00	
Accounts Payable		14,112.65	
Federal Income Tax Payable		2,103.16	
Employee Income Tax Payable		310.00	
Social Security Tax Payable		691.92	
Medicare Tax Payable		161.82	
Sales Tax Payable		6,210.66	
Unemployment Tax Payable—Federal		21.53	
Unemployment Tax Payable—State		145.29	
Health Insurance Premiums Payable		1,105.00	
Dividends Payable		5,000.00	
Total Liabilities			46,017.03
Stockholders' Equity			
Capital Stock		30,000.00	
Retained Earnings		48,198.67	
Total Stockholders' Equity			78,198.67
Total Liabilities and Stockholders' Equity			124,215.70

REINFORCEMENT ACTIVITY 3 PART B (continued)

18.

GENERAL JOURNAL PAGE 13

	DATE		ACCOUNT TITLE	DOC. NO.	POST. REF.	DEBIT	CREDIT	
1			Adjusting Entries					1
2	20-- Dec.	31	Interest Receivable		1120	24 00		2
3			Interest Income		7110		24 00	3
4		31	Uncollectible Accounts Expense		6165	3600 00		4
5			Allowance for Uncollectible Accounts		1130		3600 00	5
6		31	Merchandise Inventory		1135	6315 00		6
7			Income Summary		3120		6315 00	7
8		31	Supplies Expense		6160	2674 00		8
9			Supplies		1140		2674 00	9
10		31	Insurance Expense		6130	8000 00		10
11			Prepaid Insurance		1145		8000 00	11
12		31	Depreciation Exp.—Office Equipment		6120	6520 00		12
13			Accum. Depr.—Office Equipment		1210		6520 00	13
14		31	Depreciation Exp.—Warehouse Equipment		6125	4210 00		14
15			Accum. Depr.—Warehouse Equipment		1220		4210 00	15
16		31	Interest Expense		8105	155 00		16
17			Interest Payable		2110		155 00	17
18		31	Federal Income Tax Expense		9105	2103 16		18
19			Federal Income Tax Payable		2120		2103 16	19
20								20
21								21
22								22
23								23
24								24
25								25
26								26
27								27
28								28
29								29
30								30
31								31
32								32
33								33

Name ______________________ Date ____________ Class ____________

REINFORCEMENT ACTIVITY 3 PART B (continued)

19.

GENERAL JOURNAL PAGE 14

	DATE		ACCOUNT TITLE	DOC. NO.	POST. REF.	DEBIT	CREDIT	
1			*Closing Entries*					1
2	20-- Dec.	31	Sales		4105	779,210.90		2
3			Purchases Discount		5110	3,596.08		3
4			Purchases Returns and Allowances		5115	3,236.00		4
5			Gain on Plant Assets		7105	745.00		5
6			Interest Income		7110	438.00		6
7			Income Summary		3120		787,225.98	7
8		31	Income Summary		3120	749,231.51		8
9			Sales Discount		4110		1,889.20	9
10			Sales Returns and Allowances		4115		6,174.80	10
11			Purchases		5105		529,022.40	11
12			Advertising Expense		6105		9,606.70	12
13			Cash Short and Over		6110		20.09	13
14			Credit Card Fee Expense		6115		14,529.40	14
15			Depreciation Exp.—Office Equipment		6120		6,760.00	15
16			Depreciation Exp.—Warehouse Equip.		6125		4,650.00	16
17			Insurance Expense		6130		8,000.00	17
18			Miscellaneous Expense		6135		5,828.32	18
19			Payroll Taxes Expense		6140		10,669.44	19
20			Rent Expense		6145		21,000.00	20
21			Repairs Expense		6150		1,394.80	21
22			Salary Expense		6155		104,878.00	22
23			Supplies Expense		6160		2,674.00	23
24			Uncollectible Accounts Expense		6165		3,600.00	24
25			Utilities Expense		6170		7,236.20	25
26			Interest Expense		8105		2,905.00	26
27			Loss on Plant Assets		8110		290.00	27
28			Federal Income Tax Expense		9105		8,103.16	28
29		31	Income Summary		3120	44,309.47		29
30			Retained Earnings		3110		44,309.47	30
31		31	Retained Earnings		3110	20,000.00		31
32			Dividends		3115		20,000.00	32
33								33

REINFORCEMENT ACTIVITY 3 PART B (continued)

20.

Sparkle, Inc.

Post-Closing Trial Balance

For Year Ended December 31, 20X4

ACCOUNT TITLE	DEBIT	CREDIT
Cash	8,100.70	
Petty Cash	200.00	
Notes Receivable	3,600.00	
Interest Receivable	24.00	
Accounts Receivable	7,894.60	
Allowance for Uncollectible Accounts		2,130.60
Merchandise Inventory	80,491.95	
Supplies	425.05	
Prepaid Insurance	600.00	
Office Equipment	23,830.00	
Accumulated Depreciation—Office Equipment		13,680.00
Warehouse Equipment	26,110.00	
Accumulated Depreciation—Warehouse Equipment		11,250.00
Notes Payable		16,000.00
Interest Payable		155.00
Accounts Payable		14,112.65
Federal Income Tax Payable		2,103.16
Employee Income Tax Payable		310.00
Social Security Tax Payable		691.92
Medicare Tax Payable		161.82
Sales Tax Payable		6,210.66
Unemployment Tax Payable—Federal		21.53
Unemployment Tax Payable—State		145.29
Health Insurance Premiums Payable		1,105.00
Dividends Payable		5,000.00
Capital Stock		30,000.00
Retained Earnings		48,198.67
Totals	151,276.30	151,276.30

Name ______________ Date ______________ Class ______________

REINFORCEMENT ACTIVITY 3 PART B (concluded)

21.

GENERAL JOURNAL PAGE 15

	DATE		ACCOUNT TITLE	DOC. NO.	POST. REF.	DEBIT	CREDIT	
1			*Reversing Entries*					1
2	20-- Jan.	1	Interest Income		7110	24 00		2
3			Interest Receivable		1120		24 00	3
4		1	Interest Payable		2110	155 00		4
5			Interest Expense		8105		155 00	5
6		1	Federal Income Tax Payable		2120	2103 16		6
7			Federal Income Tax Expense		9105		2103 16	7
8								8
9								9
10								10
11								11
12								12
13								13
14								14
15								15
16								16
17								17
18								18
19								19
20								20
21								21
22								22
23								23
24								24
25								25
26								26
27								27
28								28
29								29
30								30
31								31
32								32
33								33

Study Guide 23

Name	Perfect Score	Your Score
Identifying Accounting Terms	8 Pts.	
Identifying Accounting Concepts and Practices	12 Pts.	
Analyzing Partnership Transactions	27 Pts.	
Total	47 Pts.	

Part One—Identifying Accounting Terms

Directions: Select the one term in Column I that best fits each definition in Column II. Print the letter identifying your choice in the Answers column.

Column I	Column II	Answers
A. distribution of net income statement	**1.** A business in which two or more persons combine their assets and skills. (p. 674)	1. *D*
B. owners' equity statement	**2.** Each member of a partnership. (p. 674)	2. *C*
C. partner	**3.** A written agreement setting forth the conditions under which a partnership is to operate. (p. 675)	3. *E*
D. partnership	**4.** A partnership financial statement showing net income or loss distribution to partners. (p. 680)	4. *A*
E. partnership agreement	**5.** A financial statement that summarizes the changes in owners' equity during a fiscal period. (p. 682)	5. *B*
F. liquidation of a partnership	**6.** The process of paying a partnership's liabilities and distributing remaining assets to the partners. (p. 686)	6. *F*
G. limited liability partnership (LLP)	**7.** Cash received from the sale of assets during liquidation of a partnership. (p. 686)	7. *H*
H. realization	**8.** A partnership that combines the advantages of the partnership and the corporation, while avoiding their disadvantages. (p. 688)	8. *G*

Part Two—Identifying Accounting Concepts and Practices

Directions: Place a *T* for True or an *F* for False in the Answers column to show whether each of the following statements is true or false.

		Answers
1.	In a partnership, it is not necessary to separate reports and financial records of the business from the personal records of the partners. (p. 674)	**1.** *F*
2.	During a fiscal period, partners may take assets out of the partnership in anticipation of the net income for the period. (p. 677)	**2.** *T*
3.	Withdrawals reduce the amount of a business's capital. (p. 677)	**3.** *T*
4.	The drawing accounts have normal credit balances. (p. 677)	**4.** *F*
5.	Withdrawals are normally recorded in separate accounts so that the total amounts are easily determined for each accounting period. (p. 677)	**5.** *T*
6.	A partnership's net income or net loss must be divided equally between the partners. (p. 680)	**6.** *F*
7.	The owners' equity statement enables business owners to determine if owners' equity is increasing or decreasing and what is causing the change. (p. 682)	**7.** *T*
8.	When a partnership goes out of business, any remaining cash is distributed to the partners according to each partner's total equity. (p. 686)	**8.** *T*
9.	Noncash assets cannot be sold for more than the recorded book value. (p. 687)	**9.** *F*
10.	A credit balance in the Loss and Gain on Realization account indicates a gain on realization. (p. 689)	**10.** *T*
11.	The distribution for loss or gain on realization is based on the method of distributing net income or net loss as stated in the partnership agreement. (p. 689)	**11.** *T*
12.	If there is a loss on realization, each partner's capital account is debited for the partner's share of the loss. (p. 689)	**12.** *T*

Name ______________________ Date ______________ Class ______________

Part Three—Analyzing Partnership Transactions

Directions: Analyze each of the following transactions into debit and credit parts. Print the letter identifying your choices in the proper Answers column. Determine in which journal each of the transactions is to be recorded.

G—General Journal CP—Cash Payments Journal CR—Cash Receipts Journal

Account Titles

A. Accounts Payable
B. Accumulated Depreciation—Office Equipment
C. Bruce Collinson, Capital
D. Bruce Collinson, Drawing
E. Cash
F. Katrina Welsh, Capital
G. Katrina Welsh, Drawing
H. Loss and Gain on Realization
I. Office Equipment
J. Purchases
K. Supplies

Transactions	Journal	Debit	Credit
1–2–3. Partners Katrina Welsh and Bruce Collinson each contribute cash and office equipment to the partnership. (p. 676)	1. *CR*	2. *E, I*	3. *C, F*
4–5–6. Bruce Collinson withdraws cash from the business for personal use. (p. 677)	4. *CP*	5. *D*	6. *E*
7–8–9. Katrina Welsh withdraws office equipment for personal use. (p. 678)	7. *G*	8. *G*	9. *I*
10–11–12. The partnership is liquidated, and the office equipment, costing $32,000 and having a book value of $20,000, is sold for $22,500. (p. 686)	10. *CR*	11. *B, E*	12. *H, I*
13–14–15. The partnership is liquidated, and the supplies valued at $800 are sold for $650. (p. 687)	13. *CR*	14. *E, H*	15. *K*
16–17–18. The partnership is liquidated, and cash is paid to all creditors for the amounts owed. (p. 688)	16. *CP*	17. *A*	18. *E*
19–20–21. A gain on realization is distributed to the partners. (p. 689)	19. *G*	20. *H*	21. *C, F*
22–23–24. A loss on realization is distributed to the partners. (p. 689)	22. *G*	23. *C, F*	24. *H*
25–26–27. After liquidation, the remaining cash is distributed to the partners. (p. 689)	25. *CP*	26. *C, F*	27. *E*

Name ______________________ Date ______________ Class ______________

23-1 WORK TOGETHER, p. 679

Journalizing partners' investments and withdrawals

1.

CASH RECEIPTS JOURNAL PAGE 1

	DATE		ACCOUNT TITLE	DOC. NO.	POST. REF.	1 GENERAL DEBIT	2 GENERAL CREDIT	3 ACCOUNTS RECEIVABLE CREDIT	4 SALES CREDIT	5 SALES DISCOUNT DEBIT	6 CASH DEBIT	
1	20-- Mar.	1	Office Supplies	R1		3 000 00					22 000 00	1
2			Robert Billings, Capital				25 000 00					2
3		1	Susan Billings, Capital	R2			25 000 00				25 000 00	3
4												4
5												5
6												6
7												7
8												8
9												9
10												10
11												11
12												12
13												13
14												14
15												15
16												16
17												17
18												18
19												19
20												20
21												21
22												22
23												23
24												24

2.

CASH PAYMENTS JOURNAL

PAGE 1

	DATE	ACCOUNT TITLE	CK. NO.	POST. REF.	1 GENERAL DEBIT	2 GENERAL CREDIT	3 ACCOUNTS PAYABLE DEBIT	4 PURCHASES DISCOUNT CREDIT	5 CASH CREDIT	
1	20-- Mar. 30	Susan Billings, Drawing	23		600 00				600 00	1
2										2
3										3
4										4
5										5
6										6
7										7
8										8
9										9
10										10
11										11
12										12
13										13
14										14
15										15
16										16
17										17
18										18
19										19
20										20
21										21
22										22
23										23
24										24

Name ______________ Date ______________ Class ______________

23-1 WORK TOGETHER (concluded)

2.

GENERAL JOURNAL PAGE 3

	DATE		ACCOUNT TITLE	DOC. NO.	POST. REF.	DEBIT	CREDIT	
1	20-- Mar.	30	Robert Billings, Drawing	M4		600 00		1
2			Purchases				600 00	2
3								3
4								4
5								5
6								6
7								7
8								8
9								9
10								10
11								11
12								12
13								13
14								14
15								15
16								16
17								17
18								18
19								19
20								20
21								21
22								22
23								23
24								24
25								25
26								26
27								27
28								28
29								29
30								30
31								31
32								32
33								33

23-1 ON YOUR OWN, p. 679

Journalizing partners' investments and withdrawals

1.

CASH RECEIPTS JOURNAL

PAGE 1

	DATE		ACCOUNT TITLE	DOC. NO.	POST. REF.	1 GENERAL DEBIT	2 GENERAL CREDIT	3 ACCOUNTS RECEIVABLE CREDIT	4 SALES CREDIT	5 SALES DISCOUNT DEBIT	6 CASH DEBIT	
1	20-- Sept.	1	Merchandise Inventory	R1		5 000 00					45 000 00	1
2			Loane Le, Capital				50 000 00					2
3		1	Wheatonia Makebu, Capital	R2			30 000 00				30 000 00	3
4												4
5												5
6												6
7												7
8												8
9												9
10												10
11												11
12												12
13												13
14												14
15												15
16												16
17												17
18												18
19												19
20												20
21												21
22												22
23												23
24												24

23-1 ON YOUR OWN (continued)

2.

CASH PAYMENTS JOURNAL

PAGE 1

DATE		ACCOUNT TITLE	CK. NO.	POST. REF.	1 GENERAL DEBIT	2 GENERAL CREDIT	3 ACCOUNTS PAYABLE DEBIT	4 PURCHASES DISCOUNT CREDIT	5 CASH CREDIT
20-- Sept.	30	Loane Le, Drawing	65		1 000 00				1 000 00

23-1 ON YOUR OWN (concluded)

2.

GENERAL JOURNAL PAGE 9

DATE		ACCOUNT TITLE	DOC. NO.	POST. REF.	DEBIT	CREDIT
20-- Sept.	30	*Wheatonia Makebu, Drawing*	*M6*		*1 500 00*	
		Purchases				*1 500 00*

Name ______________________ Date ____________ Class ____________

23-2 WORK TOGETHER, p. 685

Preparing distribution of net income and owners' equity statements

1.

B and B Diving

Distribution of Net Income Statement

For Month Ended March 31, 20 – –

Robert Billings	
50.0% of Net Income	14 800 00
Susan Billings	
50.0% of Net Income	14 800 00
Net Income	29 600 00

2.

B and B Diving

Owners' Equity Statement

For Month Ended March 31, 20 – –

Robert Billings			
Capital, March 1, 20 – –		25 000 00	
Share of Net Income	14 800 00		
Less Withdrawals	600 00		
Net Increase in Capital		14 200 00	
Capital, March 31, 20 – –			39 200 00
Susan Billings			
Capital, March 1, 20 – –		25 000 00	
Share of Net Income	14 800 00		
Less Withdrawals	600 00		
Net Increase in Capital		14 200 00	
Capital, March 31, 20 – –			39 200 00
Total Owners' Equity, March 31, 20 – –			78 400 00

23-2 ON YOUR OWN, p. 685

Preparing distribution of net income and owners' equity statements

1.

Northern Lights
Distribution of Net Income Statement
For Month Ended September 30, 20 – –

Loane Le	
60.0% of Net Income	35,280.00
Wheatonia Makebu	
40.0% of Net Income	23,520.00
Net Income	58,800.00

2.

Northern Lights
Owners' Equity Statement
For Month Ended September 30, 20 – –

Loane Le			
Capital, September 1, 20 – –		35,000.00	
Share of Net Income	35,280.00		
Less Withdrawals	4,500.00		
Net Increase in Capital		30,780.00	
Capital, September 30, 20 – –			65,780.00
Wheatonia Makebu			
Capital, September 1, 20 – –		28,000.00	
Share of Net Income	23,520.00		
Less Withdrawals	2,600.00		
Net Increase in Capital		20,920.00	
Capital, September 30, 20 – –			48,920.00
Total Owners' Equity, September 30, 20 – –			114,700.00

Name ______________________ Date ____________ Class ____________

23-3 WORK TOGETHER, p. 690

Liquidation of a partnership

Cash	$12,500.00
Supplies	1,250.00
Office Equipment	15,000.00
Accumulated Depreciation—Office Equipment	8,250.00
Truck	25,500.00
Accumulated Depreciation—Truck	18,300.00
Accounts Payable	1,250.00
Jason Edson, Capital	13,450.00
Peggy Karam, Capital	13,000.00

1.

GENERAL JOURNAL — PAGE 4

	DATE		ACCOUNT TITLE	DOC. NO.	POST. REF.	DEBIT	CREDIT	
1	20-- May	6	*Jason Edson, Capital*	*M21*		*450 00*		1
2			*Peggy Karam, Capital*			*300 00*		2
3			*Loss and Gain on Realization*				*750 00*	3
4								4
5								5
6								6
7								7
8								8
9								9
10								10
11								11
12								12
13								13
14								14
15								15
16								16
17								17
18								18
19								19
20								20

1.

CASH RECEIPTS JOURNAL

PAGE 6

	Date		Account Title	Doc. No.	Post. Ref.	General Debit (1)	General Credit (2)	Accounts Receivable Credit (3)	Sales Credit (4)	Sales Discount Debit (5)	Cash Debit (6)	
1	20-- May	1	Loss and Gain on Realization	R86		750 00					6,000 00	1
2			Accum. Depr.—Office Equipment			8,250 00						2
3			Office Equipment				15,000 00					3
4		1	Loss and Gain on Realization	R87		300 00					950 00	4
5			Supplies				1,250 00					5
6		3	Accum. Depr.—Truck	R88		18,300 00					7,500 00	6
7			Truck				25,500 00					7
8			Loss and Gain on Realization				300 00					8
9												9
10												10
11												11

1.

CASH PAYMENTS JOURNAL

PAGE 8

	Date		Account Title	Ck. No.	Post. Ref.	General Debit (1)	General Credit (2)	Accounts Payable Debit (3)	Cash Credit (4)	
1	20-- May	5	✓	116	✓			1,250 00	1,250 00	1
2		6	Jason Edson, Capital	117		13,000 00			13,000 00	2
3			Peggy Karam, Capital	118		12,700 00			12,700 00	3
4										4
5										5
6										6
7										7
8										8

Name ________________ Date ________ Class ________

23-3 ON YOUR OWN, p. 690

Liquidation of a partnership

Cash	$17,500.00
Supplies	1,500.00
Office Equipment	10,000.00
Accumulated Depreciation—Office Equipment	8,000.00
Truck	35,000.00
Accumulated Depreciation—Truck	30,000.00
Accounts Payable	8,000.00
Daska Madura, Capital	13,000.00
Lawrence Neary, Capital	5,000.00

1.

GENERAL JOURNAL — PAGE 5

	DATE		ACCOUNT TITLE	DOC. NO.	POST. REF.	DEBIT	CREDIT	
1	20-- June	6	*Daska Madura, Capital*	*M29*		*420 00*		1
2			*Lawrence Neary, Capital*			*280 00*		2
3			*Loss and Gain on Distribution*				*700 00*	3
4								4
5								5
6								6
7								7
8								8
9								9
10								10
11								11
12								12
13								13
14								14
15								15
16								16
17								17
18								18
19								19
20								20

23-3 ON YOUR OWN (concluded)

1.

CASH RECEIPTS JOURNAL

PAGE 8

	DATE		ACCOUNT TITLE	DOC. NO.	POST. REF.	GENERAL DEBIT (1)	GENERAL CREDIT (2)	ACCOUNTS RECEIVABLE CREDIT (3)	SALES CREDIT (4)	SALES DISCOUNT DEBIT (5)	CASH DEBIT (6)	
1	20-- June	1	Loss and Gain on Realization	R96		1 200 00					800 00	1
2			Accum. Depr.—Office Equipment			8 000 00						2
3			Office Equipment				10 000 00					3
4		1	Supplies	R97			1 500 00				1 600 00	4
5			Loss and Gain on Realization				100 00					5
6		3	Accum. Depr.—Truck	R98		30 000 00					5 400 00	6
7			Truck				35 000 00					7
8			Loss and Gain on Realization				400 00					8
9												9
10												10
11												11

1.

CASH PAYMENTS JOURNAL

PAGE 10

	DATE		ACCOUNT TITLE	CK. NO.	POST. REF.	GENERAL DEBIT (1)	GENERAL CREDIT (2)	ACCOUNTS PAYABLE DEBIT (3)	CASH CREDIT (4)	
1	20-- June	5	✔	125	✔			8 000 00	8 000 00	1
2		6	Daska Madura, Capital	126		12 580 00			12 580 00	2
3			Lawrence Neary, Capital	127		4 720 00			4 720 00	3
4										4
5										5
6										6
7										7
8										8

Name ______________________ Date ______________ Class ______________

23-1 APPLICATION PROBLEM, p. 692

Journalizing partners' investments and withdrawals

1.

CASH RECEIPTS JOURNAL PAGE 1

	DATE		ACCOUNT TITLE	DOC. NO.	POST. REF.	1 GENERAL DEBIT	2 GENERAL CREDIT	3 ACCOUNTS RECEIVABLE CREDIT	4 SALES CREDIT	5 SALES DISCOUNT DEBIT	6 CASH DEBIT	
1	20-- Apr.	1	Equipment	R1		33 000 00					2 000 00	1
2			Wilhelm Mellberg, Capital				35 000 00					2
3		1	Julie Jenson, Capital	R2			30 000 00				30 000 00	3
4												4
5												5
6												6
7												7
8												8
9												9
10												10
11												11
12												12
13												13
14												14
15												15
16												16
17												17
18												18
19												19
20												20
21												21
22												22
23												23
24												24

23-1 APPLICATION PROBLEM (continued)

2.

CASH PAYMENTS JOURNAL

PAGE 5

	DATE		ACCOUNT TITLE	CK. NO.	POST. REF.	1 GENERAL DEBIT	2 GENERAL CREDIT	3 ACCOUNTS PAYABLE DEBIT	4 PURCHASES DISCOUNT CREDIT	5 CASH CREDIT	
1	20-- Apr.	30	*Julie Jenson, Drawing*	66		3 600 00				3 600 00	1
2											2
3											3
4											4
5											5
6											6
7											7
8											8
9											9
10											10
11											11
12											12
13											13
14											14
15											15
16											16
17											17
18											18
19											19
20											20
21											21
22											22
23											23
24											24

Name ______ Date ______ Class ______

23-1 APPLICATION PROBLEM (concluded)

2.

GENERAL JOURNAL PAGE 12

	DATE		ACCOUNT TITLE	DOC. NO.	POST. REF.	DEBIT	CREDIT	
1	20-- Apr.	30	Wilhelm Mellberg, Drawing	M10		4 800 00		1
2			Purchases				4 800 00	2
3								3
4								4
5								5
6								6
7								7
8								8
9								9
10								10
11								11
12								12
13								13
14								14
15								15
16								16
17								17
18								18
19								19
20								20
21								21
22								22
23								23
24								24
25								25
26								26
27								27
28								28
29								29
30								30
31								31
32								32
33								33

23-2 APPLICATION PROBLEM, p. 692

Preparing distribution of net income and owners' equity statements (net income)

1.

Kelly Appliances
Distribution of Net Income Statement
For Year Ended December 31, 20 – –

Janet Kelly	
60.0% of Net Income	49 956 00
Paul Sharp	
40.0% of Net Income	33 304 00
Net Income	83 260 00

Name ______________________ Date ____________ Class ____________

23-2 APPLICATION PROBLEM (concluded)

2.

Kelly Appliances

Owners' Equity Statement

For Year Ended December 31, 20 – –

Janet Kelly			
Capital, January 1, 20 – –		159 000 00	
Share of Net Income	49 956 00		
Less Withdrawals	17 550 00		
Net Increase in Capital		32 406 00	
Capital, December 31, 20 – –			191 406 00
Paul Sharp			
Capital, January 1, 20 – –		142 600 00	
Share of Net Income	33 304 00		
Less Withdrawals	18 800 00		
Net Increase in Capital		14 504 00	
Capital, December 31, 20 – –			157 104 00
Total Owners' Equity, December 31, 20 – –			348 510 00

23-3 APPLICATION PROBLEM, p. 693

Preparing an owners' equity statement (net loss)

1.

Elegant Cosmetics

Owners' Equity Statement

For Year Ended December 31, 20 – –

Judy Fulton			
Capital, January 1, 20 – –	124 300 00		
Plus Additional Investment	12 000 00		
Total		136 300 00	
Share of Net Loss	3 750 00		
Plus Withdrawals	13 950 00		
Net Decrease in Capital		17 700 00	
Capital, December 31, 20 – –			118 600 00
Lee Terry			
Capital, January 1, 20 – –	118 000 00		
Plus Additional Investment	10 000 00		
Total		128 000 00	
Share of Net Loss	3 750 00		
Plus Withdrawals	14 900 00		
Net Decrease in Capital		18 650 00	
Capital, December 31, 20 – –			109 350 00
Total Owners' Equity, December 31, 20 – –			227 950 00

Name ______ Date ______ Class ______

23-4 APPLICATION PROBLEM, p. 693

Liquidating a partnership

1.

GENERAL JOURNAL PAGE 7

	DATE		ACCOUNT TITLE	DOC. NO.	POST. REF.	DEBIT	CREDIT	
1	20-- July	6	Donald Winn, Capital	M34		390 00		1
2			Judy Reed, Capital			210 00		2
3			Loss and Gain on Realization				600 00	3
4								4
5								5
6								6
7								7
8								8
9								9
10								10
11								11
12								12
13								13
14								14
15								15
16								16
17								17
18								18
19								19
20								20
21								21
22								22
23								23
24								24
25								25
26								26
27								27
28								28
29								29
30								30
31								31
32								32

23-4 APPLICATION PROBLEM (concluded)

1.

CASH RECEIPTS JOURNAL

PAGE 13

	DATE		ACCOUNT TITLE	DOC. NO.	POST. REF.	1 GENERAL DEBIT	2 GENERAL CREDIT	3 ACCOUNTS RECEIVABLE CREDIT	4 SALES CREDIT	5 SALES DISCOUNT DEBIT	6 CASH DEBIT	
1	20-- July	1	Loss and Gain on Realization	R114		500 00					400 00	1
2			Accum. Depr.—Office Equipment			5 500 00						2
3			Office Equipment				10 000 00					3
4		1	Loss and Gain on Realization	R115		300 00					200 00	4
5			Supplies				500 00					5
6		3	Accum. Depr.—Truck	R116		12 200 00					5 000 00	6
7			Truck				17 000 00					7
8			Loss and Gain on Realization				200 00					8
9												9
10												10
11												11

1.

CASH PAYMENTS JOURNAL

PAGE 13

	DATE		ACCOUNT TITLE	CK. NO.	POST. REF.	1 GENERAL DEBIT	2 GENERAL CREDIT	3 ACCOUNTS PAYABLE DEBIT	4 PURCHASES DISCOUNT CREDIT	5 CASH CREDIT	
1	20-- July	5	✓	156	✓			500 00		500 00	1
2		6	Donald Winn, Capital	157		6 910 00				6 910 00	2
3			Judy Reed, Capital	158		6 790 00				6 790 00	3
4											4
5											5
6											6
7											7
8											8

Name ______________________ Date ______________ Class ______________

23-5 MASTERY PROBLEM, pp. 694, 695

Recording partners' investments and withdrawals, preparing financial statements, and liquidating a partnership

1., 5.

CASH RECEIPTS JOURNAL PAGE 13

	DATE	ACCOUNT TITLE	DOC. NO.	POST. REF.	1 GENERAL DEBIT	2 GENERAL CREDIT	3 ACCOUNTS RECEIVABLE CREDIT	4 SALES CREDIT	5 SALES DISCOUNT DEBIT	6 CASH DEBIT	
1	20-- July 15	Darren Greenlund, Capital	R87			10 000 00				10 000 00	1
2	15	Equipment	R88		8 000 00					3 000 00	2
3		Karen Greenlund, Capital				11 000 00					3
4	31	Loss and Gain on Realization	R89		2 0 0 00					1 8 0 0 00	4
5		Merchandise Inventory				2 000 00					5
6	31	Accum. Depr.—Equipment	R90		10 000 00					7 000 00	6
7		Equipment				15 000 00					7
8		Loss and Gain on Realization				2 000 00					8
9											9
10											10
11											11
12											12
13											13
14											14
15											15
16											16
17											17
18											18
19											19
20											20
21											21
22											22
23											23
24											24

23-5 MASTERY PROBLEM (continued)

2., 5.

CASH PAYMENTS JOURNAL — PAGE 19

	DATE		ACCOUNT TITLE	CK. NO.	POST. REF.	1 GENERAL DEBIT	2 GENERAL CREDIT	3 ACCOUNTS PAYABLE DEBIT	4 PURCHASES DISCOUNT CREDIT	5 CASH CREDIT	
1	20-- July	31	Darren Greenlund, Drawing	321		800 00				800 00	1
2		31	✓	322				2500 00		2500 00	2
3		31	Darren Greenlund, Capital	323		49710 00				49710 00	3
4		31	Karen Greenlund, Capital	324		47080 00				47080 00	4
5											5
6											6
7											7
8											8
9											9
10											10
11											11
12											12
13											13
14											14
15											15
16											16
17											17
18											18
19											19
20											20
21											21
22											22
23											23
24											24

Name ______________________ Date ______________ Class ______________

23-5 MASTERY PROBLEM (continued)

2., 5.

GENERAL JOURNAL PAGE 23

	DATE		ACCOUNT TITLE	DOC. NO.	POST. REF.	DEBIT	CREDIT	
1	20-- July	31	Karen Greenlund, Drawing	M61		1 000 00		1
2			Purchases				1 000 00	2
3		31	Loss and Gain on Realization	M62		1 800 00		3
4			Darren Greenlund, Capital				900 00	4
5			Karen Greenlund, Capital				900 00	5
6								6
7								7
8								8
9								9
10								10
11								11
12								12
13								13
14								14
15								15
16								16
17								17
18								18
19								19
20								20
21								21
22								22
23								23
24								24
25								25
26								26
27								27
28								28
29								29
30								30
31								31
32								32
33								33

3.

GreenGarden

Distribution of Net Income Statement

For Month Ended July 31, 20 – –

Darren Greenlund	
50.0% of Net Income	7,300.00
Karen Greenlund	
50.0% of Net Income	7,300.00
Net Income	14,600.00

23-5 MASTERY PROBLEM (concluded)

4.

GreenGarden

Owners' Equity Statement

For Month Ended July 31, 20 – –

Darren Greenlund			
Capital, July 1, 20 – –	32 3 1 0 00		
Plus Additional Investment	10 0 0 0 00		
Total		42 3 1 0 00	
Share of Net Income	7 3 0 0 00		
Less Withdrawals	8 0 0 00		
Increase in Capital		6 5 0 0 00	
Capital, July 31, 20 – –			48 8 1 0 00
Karen Greenlund			
Capital, July 1, 20 – –	28 8 8 0 00		
Plus Additional Investment	11 0 0 0 00		
Total		39 8 8 0 00	
Share of Net Income	7 3 0 0 00		
Less Withdrawals	1 0 0 0 00		
Increase in Capital		6 3 0 0 00	
Capital, July 31, 20 – –			46 1 8 0 00
Total Owners' Equity, July 31, 20 – –			94 9 9 0 00

23-6 CHALLENGE PROBLEM, p. 695

Preparing a distribution of net income statement and owners' equity statement (unequal distribution of net loss; additional investment)

1.

Jewelry Joint

Distribution of Net Income Statement

For Year Ended December 31, 20 – –

Kaye Skousen	
65.0% of Net Loss	*21 0 2 1 00*
Timothy Tripp	
35.0% of Net Loss	*11 3 1 9 00*
Net Loss	*32 3 4 0 00*

Name ____________________ Date ____________ Class ____________

23-6 CHALLENGE PROBLEM (concluded)

2.

Jewelry Joint

Owners' Equity Statement

For Year Ended December 31, 20 – –

Kaye Skousen			
Capital, January 1, 20 – –	125,294.00		
Plus Additional Investment	11,000.00		
Total		136,294.00	
Share of Net Loss	21,021.00		
Plus Withdrawals	18,000.00		
Net Decrease in Capital		39,021.00	
Capital, December 31, 20 – –			97,273.00
Timothy Tripp			
Capital, January 1, 20 – –	101,961.00		
Plus Additional Investment	9,500.00		
Total		111,461.00	
Share of Net Loss	11,319.00		
Plus Withdrawals	16,300.00		
Net Decrease in Capital		27,619.00	
Capital, December 31, 20 – –			83,842.00
Total Owners' Equity, December 31, 20 – –			181,115.00

Study Guide 24

Name	Perfect Score	Your Score
Identifying Accounting Terms	10 Pts.	
Analyzing International and Internet Sales	10 Pts.	
Analyzing Accounts Affected by International and Internet Transactions	12 Pts.	
Total	32 Pts.	

Part One—Identifying Accounting Terms

Directions: Select the one term in Column I that best fits each definition in Column II. Print the letter identifying your choice in the Answers column.

Column I	Column II	Answers
A. bill of lading	**1.** Goods or services shipped out of a seller's home country to a foreign country. (p. 702)	1. *E*
B. commercial invoice	**2.** Goods or services bought from a foreign country and brought into a buyer's home country. (p. 702)	2. *F*
C. contract of sale	**3.** A document that details all the terms agreed to by seller and buyer for a sales transaction. (p. 703)	3. *C*
D. draft	**4.** A letter issued by a bank guaranteeing that a named individual or business will be paid a specified amount provided stated conditions are met. (p. 703)	4. *G*
E. exports	**5.** A receipt signed by the authorized agent of a transportation company for merchandise received that also serves as a contract for the delivery of the merchandise. (p. 704)	5. *A*
F. imports	**6.** A statement prepared by the seller of merchandise addressed to the buyer showing a detailed listing and description of merchandise sold, including price and terms. (p. 704)	6. *B*
G. letter of credit	**7.** A written, signed, and dated order from one party ordering another party, usually a bank, to pay money to a third party. (p. 704)	7. *D*
H. sight draft	**8.** A draft payable on sight when the holder presents it for payment. (p. 704)	8. *H*
I. time draft	**9.** A draft that is payable at a fixed or determinable future time after it is accepted. (p. 707)	9. *I*
J. trade acceptance	**10.** A form signed by a buyer at the time of a sale of merchandise in which the buyer promises to pay the seller a specified sum of money, usually at a stated time in the future. (p. 708)	10. *J*

Part Two—Analyzing International and Internet Sales

Directions: Place a *T* for True or an *F* for False in the Answers column to show whether each of the following statements is true or false.

		Answers
1.	International sales are just as simple as domestic sales. (p. 702)	**1.** *F*
2.	All transactions in the United States are covered by the same universal commercial laws and the same accounting standards. (p. 703)	**2.** *T*
3.	The risk of uncollected amounts is increased with international sales. (p. 703)	**3.** *T*
4.	A draft is sometimes referred to as a bank exchange. (p. 704)	**4.** *F*
5.	Sales taxes are normally paid only on sales to the final consumer. (p. 706)	**5.** *T*
6.	A seller generally has much more assurance of receiving payment from a buyer than from a bank. (p. 708)	**6.** *F*
7.	Most businesses use trade acceptances in international sales. (p. 708)	**7.** *F*
8.	Companies that sell on the Internet must be able to accept credit card sales. (p. 710)	**8.** *T*
9.	The terminal summary is used as the source document for Internet sales. (p. 710)	**9.** *T*
10.	Credit card sales are not considered to be cash sales. (p. 711)	**10.** *F*

Name ________________ Date ________ Class ________

Part Three—Analyzing Accounts Affected by International and Internet Transactions

Directions: Analyze each of the following transactions into debit and credit parts. Print the letter identifying your choices in the proper Answers column. Determine in which journal each of the transactions is to be recorded.

G—General Journal CP—Cash Payments Journal CR—Cash Receipts Journal

Account Titles	Transactions	Journal	Answers Debit	Credit
A. Cash	**1–2–3.** Recorded an international cash sale. (p. 706)	1. *CR*	2. *A*	3. *B*
B. Sales	**4–5–6.** Received a time draft for an international sale. (p. 707)	4. *G*	5. *C*	6. *B*
C. Time Drafts Receivable	**7–8–9.** Received cash for the value of a time draft. (p. 708)	7. *CR*	8. *A*	9. *C*
	10–11–12. Recorded Internet credit card sales. (p. 711)	10. *CR*	11. *A*	12. *B*

Study Skills

Preparing for Examinations

Some students seem to make poor grades anytime they take an examination. They say, "Taking an exam has always been impossible for me. I am not able to work well when there is any pressure." What they often actually mean is that they are unprepared for the exam.

Because you will take so many examinations in the future, you should do anything you can to become proficient in taking them. It is just good insurance for your future success.

Prepare Every Day

The best way to prepare for an exam is to complete every day's assignment on time. If you do, reviewing for an exam will be easy. You can review material the day before an exam, but you cannot make up for a term of neglect.

Find out when your next exam will be and pace your study so that you will have all work completed well before the exam. If there are review questions at the end of the chapters in your text, read them to determine if you know the answers. In this way, you will know if you understand the material.

Prepare Personally

You should make every effort to be prepared personally for an exam. Getting proper rest before the exam is essential. A student who arrives at the exam room sleepy and tired will not be able to do good work. Do not stay up late the evening before an exam even if you feel you need the time to study. To do well on an exam, you must be well rested and alert.

You should try to keep personal problems from interfering with your study or with your preparation for an exam. If you are concerned about a personal problem, it is difficult to concentrate your efforts on preparing for an exam.

Necessary Supplies

On the day of the exam, be sure that you have all the necessary supplies. You will likely need pens, pencils, and paper. Sometimes a special exam notebook is required.

It is a very good idea to take a watch with you to the exam so that you will be able to check the time regularly. In this way, you will not spend too much time on one part of the exam and fail to finish the entire exam.

Be Confident

If you are properly prepared, you can actually look forward to exams. Good preparation will help you to present your ideas and knowledge in the best possible way. Plan for exams and face them with confidence. You will be proud of yourself, and you will very likely make much better grades.

Name ______________________ Date ____________ Class ____________

24-1 WORK TOGETHER, p. 709

Journalizing international sales transactions

1., 2.

CASH RECEIPTS JOURNAL — PAGE 9

	DATE		ACCOUNT TITLE	DOC. NO.	POST. REF.	1 GENERAL DEBIT	2 GENERAL CREDIT	3 ACCOUNTS RECEIVABLE CREDIT	4 SALES CREDIT	5 SALES DISCOUNT DEBIT	6 CASH DEBIT	
1	20-- May	1	✓	M323	✓				14 000 00		14 000 00	1
2		9	Time Drafts Receivable	R221			21 000 00				21 000 00	2
3		31	Totals			—	21 000 00	—	14 000 00	—	35 000 00	3
4												4
5												5
6												6
7												7
8												8
9												9
10												10

1.

GENERAL JOURNAL — PAGE 5

	DATE		ACCOUNT TITLE	DOC. NO.	POST. REF.	DEBIT	CREDIT	
1	20-- May	5	Time Drafts Receivable	TD32		18 000 00		1
2			Sales				18 000 00	2
3								3
4								4
5								5
6								6

24-1 ON YOUR OWN, p. 709

Journalizing international sales transactions

1., 2.

CASH RECEIPTS JOURNAL PAGE 17

	DATE		ACCOUNT TITLE	DOC. NO.	POST. REF.	1 GENERAL DEBIT	2 GENERAL CREDIT	3 ACCOUNTS RECEIVABLE CREDIT	4 SALES CREDIT	5 SALES DISCOUNT DEBIT	6 CASH DEBIT	
1	20-- Sept.	3	✔	M256	✔				9 400 00		9 400 00	1
2		6	Time Drafts Receivable	R211			13 500 00				13 500 00	2
3		30	Totals			—	13 500 00	—	9 400 00	—	22 900 00	3
4												4
5												5
6												6
7												7
8												8
9												9
10												10

1.

GENERAL JOURNAL PAGE 9

	DATE		ACCOUNT TITLE	DOC. NO.	POST. REF.	DEBIT	CREDIT	
1	20-- Sept.	5	Time Drafts Receivable	TD81		7 800 00		1
2			Sales				7 800 00	2
3								3
4								4
5								5
6								6

Name ______________________ Date ____________ Class ____________

24-2 WORK TOGETHER p. 712

Journalizing Internet sales transactions

1.

CASH RECEIPTS JOURNAL — PAGE 5

	DATE		ACCOUNT TITLE	DOC. NO.	POST. REF.	1 GENERAL DEBIT	2 GENERAL CREDIT	3 ACCOUNTS RECEIVABLE CREDIT	4 SALES CREDIT	5 SALES DISCOUNT DEBIT	6 CASH DEBIT	
1	20-- Mar.	5	✓	TS331	✓				2432 00		2432 00	1
2		12	✓	TS332	✓				3010 00		3010 00	2
3		19	✓	TS333	✓				1550 00		1550 00	3
4												4
5												5
6												6
7												7
8												8
9												9
10												10
11												11
12												12
13												13
14												14
15												15
16												16
17												17
18												18
19												19
20												20
21												21
22												22

24-2 ON YOUR OWN, p. 712

Journalizing Internet sales transactions

1.

CASH RECEIPTS JOURNAL PAGE 9

	DATE		ACCOUNT TITLE	DOC. NO.	POST. REF.	1 GENERAL DEBIT	2 GENERAL CREDIT	3 ACCOUNTS RECEIVABLE CREDIT	4 SALES CREDIT	5 SALES DISCOUNT DEBIT	6 CASH DEBIT	
1	20-- May	7	✔	TS44	✔				352 00		352 00	1
2		12	✔	TS45	✔				187 00		187 00	2
3		20	✔	TS46	✔				319 00		319 00	3
4												4
5												5
6												6
7												7
8												8
9												9
10												10
11												11
12												12
13												13
14												14
15												15
16												16
17												17
18												18
19												19
20												20
21												21
22												22

Name ______________________ Date ______________ Class ______________

24-1 APPLICATION PROBLEM, p. 714

Journalizing international sales transactions

1., 2.

CASH RECEIPTS JOURNAL

PAGE 10

DATE		ACCOUNT TITLE	DOC. NO.	POST. REF.	1 GENERAL DEBIT	2 GENERAL CREDIT	3 ACCOUNTS RECEIVABLE CREDIT	4 SALES CREDIT	5 SALES DISCOUNT DEBIT	6 CASH DEBIT
20-- June	1	✓	M82	✓				12 000 00		12 000 00
	9	Time Drafts Receivable	R116			16 000 00				16 000 00
	19	Time Drafts Receivable	R117			22 000 00				22 000 00
	21	✓	M83	✓				17 500 00		17 500 00
	30	Totals			—	38 000 00	—	29 500 00	—	67 500 00

24-1 APPLICATION PROBLEM (concluded)

1.

GENERAL JOURNAL PAGE 6

	DATE		ACCOUNT TITLE	DOC. NO.	POST. REF.	DEBIT	CREDIT	
1	20-- June	5	Time Drafts Receivable	TD32		13 000 00		1
2			Sales				13 000 00	2
3		12	Time Drafts Receivable	TD33		8 000 00		3
4			Sales				8 000 00	4
5		25	Time Drafts Receivable	TD34		24 000 00		5
6			Sales				24 000 00	6
7								7
8								8
9								9
10								10
11								11
12								12
13								13
14								14
15								15
16								16
17								17
18								18
19								19
20								20
21								21
22								22
23								23
24								24
25								25
26								26
27								27
28								28
29								29
30								30
31								31
32								32
33								33

Name ______________________ Date ______________ Class ______________

24-2 APPLICATION PROBLEM, p. 714

Journalizing Internet sales transactions

1., 2.

CASH RECEIPTS JOURNAL PAGE 15

	DATE		ACCOUNT TITLE	DOC. NO.	POST. REF.	1 GENERAL DEBIT	2 GENERAL CREDIT	3 ACCOUNTS RECEIVABLE CREDIT	4 SALES CREDIT	5 SALES DISCOUNT DEBIT	6 CASH DEBIT	
1	20-- Aug.	6	✓	TS116	✓				909 00		909 00	1
2		13	✓	TS117	✓				1 480 00		1 480 00	2
3		20	✓	TS118	✓				1 147 00		1 147 00	3
4		27	✓	TS119	✓				2 843 00		2 843 00	4
5		31	*Totals*			—	—	—	6 379 00	—	6 379 00	5
6												6
7												7
8												8
9												9
10												10
11												11
12												12
13												13
14												14
15												15
16												16
17												17
18												18
19												19
20												20
21												21
22												22

24-3 MASTERY PROBLEM, p. 715

Recording international and Internet sales

1., 2.

CASH RECEIPTS JOURNAL — PAGE 2

	Date		Account Title	Doc. No.	Post. Ref.	1 General Debit	2 General Credit	3 Accounts Receivable Credit	4 Sales Credit	5 Sales Discount Debit	6 Cash Debit	
1	20-- Feb.	8	✓	TS23	✓				12 300 00		12 300 00	1
2		12	✓	M8	✓				10 500 00		10 500 00	2
3		14	Time Drafts Receivable	R35			23 000 00				23 000 00	3
4		18	✓	TS24	✓				18 400 00		18 400 00	4
5		21	Time Drafts Receivable	R37			8 000 00				8 000 00	5
6		24	✓	M12	✓				13 500 00		13 500 00	6
7		27	✓	TS25	✓				9 200 00		9 200 00	7
8		28	Totals			—	31 000 00	—	63 900 00	—	94 900 00	8
9												9
10												10
11												11
12												12
13												13
14												14
15												15
16												16
17												17
18												18
19												19
20												20
21												21
22												22

Name ____________ Date ________ Class ________

24-3 MASTERY PROBLEM (concluded)

1.

GENERAL JOURNAL PAGE 2

	DATE		ACCOUNT TITLE	DOC. NO.	POST. REF.	DEBIT	CREDIT	
1	20-- Feb.	5	*Time Drafts Receivable*	*TD10*		*5 000 00*		1
2			*Sales*				*5 000 00*	2
3		28	*Time Drafts Receivable*	*TD11*		*6 000 00*		3
4			*Sales*				*6 000 00*	4
5								5
6								6
7								7
8								8
9								9
10								10
11								11
12								12
13								13
14								14
15								15
16								16
17								17
18								18
19								19
20								20
21								21
22								22
23								23
24								24
25								25
26								26
27								27
28								28
29								29
30								30
31								31
32								32
33								33

24-4 CHALLENGE PROBLEM, p. 715

Recording international sales and converting foreign currency

1., 2.

CASH RECEIPTS JOURNAL — PAGE 11

		1	2	3	4	5	6	
	DATE		ACCOUNT TITLE	DOC. NO.	POST. REF.	GENERAL DEBIT	GENERAL CREDIT	ACCOUNTS RECEIVABLE CREDIT	SALES CREDIT	SALES DISCOUNT DEBIT	CASH DEBIT	
1	20-- June	1	✓	M46	✓				849 94		849 94	1
2		8	✓	M49	✓				1 200 00		1 200 00	2
3		14	✓	M55	✓				949 75		949 75	3
4		19	✓	M57	✓				449 26		449 26	4
5		28	✓	M68	✓				600 00		600 00	5
6		30	Totals			—	—	—	4 048 95	—	4 048 95	6
7												7
8												8
9												9
10												10
11												11
12												12

June 1: 7,026 yuan ÷ 8.26650 = $849.94 U.S.
8: 13,782 pesos ÷ 11.485 = $1,200.00 U.S.
14: $1,364 NZ ÷ 1.43616 = $949.75 U.S.
19: 354 euros ÷ .78796 = $449.26 U.S.
28: $3,174,060 Zimbabwe ÷ 5,290.10 = $600.00 U.S.

Name ______________________ Date ____________ Class ____________

PRACTICE PROBLEM A-1, p. A-6

Preparing a statement of cash flows

Bonita Body Shop

Statement of Cash Flows

For Year Ended December 31, 20 – –

Cash Flows from Operating Activities:			
Net Income		15 495 00	
Adjustments to Net Income:			
Depreciation Expense	2 300 00		
Changes in current assets and liabilities:			
Increase in accounts receivable	(1 800 00)		
Decrease in prepaid insurance	1 000 00		
Increase in accounts payable	2 500 00		
Decrease in interest payable	(1 400 00)		
Total adjustments to net income		2 600 00	
Net cash flows from operating activities			18 095 00
Cash Flows from Investing Activities:			
Purchased equipment		(4 000 00)	
Net cash flows from investing activities			(4 000 00)
Cash Flows from Financing Activities:			
Repayment of loans payable		(30 000 00)	
Dividend payment		(3 000 00)	
Net cash flows from financing activities			(33 000 00)
Net Change in Cash			(18 905 00)
Cash Balance, Beginning of Period			70 700 00
Cash Balance, End of Period			51 795 00

PRACTICE PROBLEM A-2, p. A-6

Preparing a statement of cash flows

Terrace Yard Care

Statement of Cash Flows

For Year Ended December 31, 20 – –

Cash Flows from Operating Activities:			
Net Income		3500 00	
Adjustments to Net Income:			
Depreciation Expense	2000 00		
Changes in current assets and liabilities:			
Increase in accounts receivable	(5400 00)		
Decrease in supplies	300 00		
Decrease in accounts payable	(2000 00)		
Increase in salaries payable	800 00		
Total adjustments to net income		(4300 00)	
Net cash flows from operating activities			(800 00)
Cash Flows from Investing Activities:			
Purchased equipment		(1500 00)	
Sold land		2000 00	
Net cash flows from investing activities			500 00
Cash Flows from Financing Activities:			
Proceeds from loan payable		3000 00	
Dividend payment		(1000 00)	
Net cash flows from financing activities			2000 00
Net Change in Cash			1700 00
Cash Balance, Beginning of Period			13300 00
Cash Balance, End of Period			15000 00